6/04

PLAYS FOR PERFORMANCE

A series designed for
contemporary prod
Edite
Nicholas Rudall an

D0647365

St. Louis Community College
at Meramec
Library

From the Novel by

MARY SHELLEY

Frankenstein

In a New Adaptation by
Dorothy Louise

Ivan R. Dee
CHICAGO

FRANKENSTEIN. Copyright © 2004 by Ivan R. Dee, Inc. Adaptation copyright © 2004 by Dorothy Louise. All rights reserved, including the right to reproduce this book or portions thereof in any form. For information, address the publisher at 1332 North Halsted Street, Chicago 60622. Manufactured in the United States of America and printed on acid-free paper.

CAUTION: Professionals and amateurs are hereby warned that this edition of FRANKENSTEIN is subject to a royalty. It is fully protected under the copyright laws of the United States of America and of all countries covered by the International Copyright Union (including the British Commonwealth and Canada), and of all countries covered by the Pan-American Copyright Convention and the Universal Copyright Convention, and of all countries with which the United States has reciprocal copyright relations. All rights, including professional, amateur, motion pictures, recitation, public reading, radio broadcasting, television, video or sound taping, all other forms of mechanical or electronic reproduction, and the rights of translation into foreign languages are strictly reserved.

All inquiries concerning performance rights should be addressed to Samuel French, Inc., 45 West 25th Street, New York, NY 10010, in advance of anticipated production.

Copying from this book in whole or in part is strictly forbidden by law, and the right of performance is not transferable.

Library of Congress Cataloging-in-Publication Data:
Louise, Dorothy.
    Frankenstein / from the novel by Mary Shelley ; in a new adaptation by Dorothy Louise.
        p. cm. — (Plays for performance)
    ISBN 1-56663-553-5 (alk. paper)
        1. Frankenstein (Fictitious character)—Drama. 2. Scientists—Drama. 3. Monsters—Drama. I. Shelley, Mary Wollstonecraft, 1797–1851. Frankenstein. II. Title. III. Series.

PS3612.O8F73 2004
812'.6—dc22   2003060234

INTRODUCTION

by Dorothy Louise

Out of loyalty to Mary Shelley's memory and admiration for her work, I have tried to honor in this stage adaptation the thrust of her tale, which has so often been distorted or ignored in various versions, particularly films. The heart of the distortion rests in transforming the more neutrally named "Creature" into a monster, flattening Shelley's more complex tale into a simplistic story of horror and caution. In the 1931 Boris Karloff film, a "criminal brain" accounts for the Creature's inhumanity. Shelley's story, however, centers in the Creature's gradual growth into malignity via the path of continual rejection and horrified reaction he experiences, and his creator Victor Frankenstein's ultimate refusal to respond to his very human needs. As the Creature himself, begging for a mate, says, "I am malicious because I am miserable." Society shares responsibility with Victor Frankenstein for having shaped, through revulsion and neglect, this finally malevolent product. And because neither Victor nor society will take up that responsibility, the Creature continues down a road of murder and mayhem. If this is the cliché of the noble savage, so be it.

One begins exploring Shelley's myth by examining her introduction to the novel. She centers her tale in the suffering Creature's version, wrapped in

Victor Frankenstein's narrative told to Captain Walton, itself enveloped in Captain Walton's letters to his sister conveying the whole story. But first Shelley introduces it all with the mysterious circumstances of its composition.

Surveying her writing life, Shelley notes her early tendency to imagine characters different from those whom she actually knew. In other words, she exercised early a habit of empathy, the very quality denied the Creature. She "did not make myself the heroine of my tales" because "I was not confined to my own identity, and I could people the hours with creations far more interesting to me at that age than my own sensations." As neighbors of Lord Byron on a summer visit to Switzerland in 1816, she and her lover, Percy Bysshe Shelley, found the June weather wet and "ungenial," and amused themselves with ghost stories. The three, gathering with Byron's physician, Polidori, decided that each would try to invent a ghost story. "I thought and pondered—vainly," Mary writes. Simultaneously she listened to Shelley and Byron discuss various philosophical doctrines, including "the nature of the principle of life." Then, as surely as Coleridge dreamed his *Kublai Khan*, Mary Shelley dreamed her *Frankenstein*: "I did not sleep, nor could I be said to think. My imagination, unbidden, possessed and guided me, . . . I saw the pale student of unhallowed arts kneeling beside the thing he had put together."

As vividly, she also saw Frankenstein's creation: ". . . the hideous phantasm of a man stretched out, and then, on the working of some powerful engine, show signs of life and stir with an uneasy, half-vital motion. . . . His success would terrify the artist; . . . he might sleep in the belief that the silence of the grave would quench forever the transient existence

4

of the hideous corpse which he had looked upon as the cradle of life. . . . Behold, the horrid thing stands at his bedside, opening his curtains and looking on him with yellow, watery, but speculative eyes."

Terrified herself, Shelley feels a "thrill of fear," and cannot shake the afterimage of her "hideous phantom." She then hits upon contriving a ghost story that would strike the same fear in her reader. So begins nearly two hundred years of this original and its own hideous progeny, a perennially fascinating gothic myth appealing to human daring and courage, to the risk of unleashing forces that cannot be reined in, and to the resulting responsibilities that will arise if one succeeds.

Victor Frankenstein describes his thirst for scientific knowledge to Captain Walton as "an almost supernatural enthusiasm" to answer the "bold question," "Whence . . . did the principle of life proceed?" At this stage of his mission, he shows boldness in confronting the question, noting "yet with how many things are we upon the brink of becoming acquainted, if cowardice or carelessness did not restrain our inquiries." This thought is enough to push him forward. "After days and nights of incredible labour and fatigue, . . . I became myself capable of bestowing animation upon lifeless matter." Here is both the triumph and the caution of Shelley's "modern Prometheus," who relies solely on science to guide him in his quest. Victor withholds the details from Walton, countering his earlier point against cowardice by arguing now that such knowledge is "dangerous," and "how much happier that man is who believes his native town to be the world, than he who aspires to become greater than his nature will allow."

Shelley's "modern Prometheus" myth continues to

exercise contemporary influence. Watson and Crick published their paper on the structure of DNA in April 1953, and since then further research has led to the cloning of sheep, pigs, and house cats as well as debates on the ethics of human cloning; the mapping of the human genome; human embryonic stem-cell research aimed at therapies for such diseases as Parkinson's and Alzheimer's; and genetically manipulated crops. The desire to fathom the secret of life, and by implication to gain some influence on the mystery of mortality, continues to fascinate, and its applications are commonly reported in the media. Although these advances may make Victor's method of assembling body parts and then electrifying them into life laughable, they also make his impulse understandable, even familiar.

Further, this familiarity leads us to respond to Victor's hubris in abandoning his creation. The Promethean rebel who defies tyranny and champions the oppressed appeals for his or her fearlessness, daring, ambition, and perseverance. Is it hubris or humility in Victor to think he is "destined for greatness," and to want "to be useful to my fellows"? In ranking himself "above the herd," is he not being accurate? Lucifer, Prometheus, Oedipus, Faust—the best are always drawn to overstep. Their myths involve a challenge to omniscience, a rebellious streak in our human nature. *Frankenstein* fits into this tradition, even as it mines melodrama's possibilities and transmutes them into fundamental archetypes that approach the tragic. Its appeal to pity and fear partly accounts for its endurance for nearly two centuries. Having dared to extend the boundaries of knowledge, Victor Frankenstein assumes some of the power of the tragic protagonist. And we feel the pull of the "bold question": like Walton, even knowing the unintended consequences, we would "give any-thing" to know Victor's method.

In staging this adaptation, the director would do well to consider various techniques of story theatre, with the actors playing multiple roles, creating sound effects, and even helping to suggest locales. Even trimmed to its essentials, there remains a fair amount of narrative, requiring quick changes of situation and setting best established by the actors themselves. As story theatre, the piece invites a strong directorial imagination and a bold visual/architectural idea, and therefore provides intriguing possibilities for the collaboration of director and designers. Even working at the level of a staged reading, one can easily commandeer the usual tools one finds in college and community theaters' wings and shops: scaffolding, rolling ladders, spiral staircases, and catwalks. These skeletal forms lend themselves appropriately by linking architectural elements to *Frankenstein*'s content, and they boast the added bonus of economy, flexibility, and versatility. The piece also invites an inventive sound design which would ideally include new music: and its gothic melodramatic effects should be enhanced with bold choices in lighting and video. Let the stage reclaim the cinematic thrust of this tale through such economical means, thus underlining the story's ultimate simplicity while retaining its complex ideas.

Finally, a note about research that may be especially useful to evolving the mise-en-scène. The three references listed below are all helpful in different ways: Susan Lederer curated the National Library of Medicine's 1997 exhibit, and her catalog includes many visual representations that will lead to other sources; Levine and Knoepflmacher offer various literary approaches to the novel as well as further progeny (in film, for instance); and Turney examines many key issues relevant to current ethical and scientific debates.

Susan E. Lederer, *Frankenstein: Penetrating the Secrets of Nature.* New Brunswick, N.J.: Rutgers University Press, 2002.

George Levine and U. C. Knoepflmacher, eds., *The Endurance of Frankenstein.* Berkeley: University of California Press, 1979.

Jon Turney, *Frankenstein's Footsteps: Science, Genetics and Popular Culture.* New Haven: Yale University Press, 1998.

CHARACTERS

MARY SHELLEY, *variously age sixteen to forty*
BYRON
GODWIN, *Mary's father*
VICTOR FRANKENSTEIN, *in his twenties*
ALPHONSE, *his father*
HENRY CLERVAL, *his friend*
CAROLINE, *his mother*
JUSTINE, *her ward*
PROFESSOR KREMPE
PROFESSOR WALDMAN
CREATURE, *androgynous*
ELIZABETH LAVENZA, *Victor's sister by adoption, eventually his wife*
JUSTINE MORITZ
DELACEY, *an old blind man*
WILLIAM, *Victor's younger brother*
CAPTAIN WALTON
VARIOUS EXTRAS

(Many of the smaller roles may be doubled.)

Frankenstein

ACT 1

Open space, vaguely constructivist, with scaffolding, ladders, double-helix spiral staircases, ship's rigging, and other skeletal forms.

Scene 1

A young woman, decked out in layers of Victorian finery, topples over from its weight, revealing a large baby doll. Sounds of newborn crying, signaling life. Crossfade to Mary, about forty, a shawl pulled around her shoulders, at her writing desk, firelight flickering, candle burning brightly. Godwin writes at his desk.

MARY: As a child, I scribbled . . . like my father.

GODWIN: Some novels are not meant for Lydia Languish.

(portrait of Mary Wollstonecraft projected)

MARY: Like my mother, too. She died when I was two weeks old, so I know of her scribbling only by hearsay.

GODWIN: Novels can reach the heights of poetry.

MARY: My dreams were at once more fantastic and agreeable than my writings. . . . I accounted for them to nobody; they were my refuge when annoyed—my dearest pleasure when free.

GODWIN: They can captivate the reader and so shape his feeling and opinion that he emerges from his reading changed, charged, ready to oppose the wicked and shoulder the infirm.

MARY: I could not figure to myself that romantic woes or wonderful events would ever be my lot; but I was not confined to my own identity, and I could people the hours with creations far more interesting to me at that age than my own sensations.

After this my life became busier, and reality stood in place of fiction. My husband . . . was . . . very anxious that I should prove myself worthy of my parentage and enroll myself on the page of fame . . . forever inciting me to obtain literary reputation. Still I did nothing. . . . In the summer of 1816 we visited Switzerland . . . a wet, ungenial summer, and incessant rain confined us for days to the house. . . .

(SFX, wind and rain)

BYRON: We will each write a ghost story.

MARY: I busied myself to think of a story . . . that would speak to the mysterious fears of our nature and awaken thrilling horror—make the reader dread to look around, a story to curdle the blood and quicken the beatings of the heart. . . . I felt that blank capability of invention . . . when dull Nothing replies to our anxious invocations.

REVERBERATING VOICES: Have you thought of a story? Have you thought of a story? Have you . . . ?!

BYRON: That lecture on the experiments of Dr. Darwin . . . , the bit about the pasta. *(laughs)* He preserved a piece of vermicelli in a glass case until by some extraordinary means, who knows the devil what, it began to move of its own volition—do you believe it?!

MARY: Perhaps a corpse would be reanimated; perhaps the components of a creature.... Night waned upon this talk ... my imagination, unbidden, possessed and guided me ... with a vividness far beyond the usual bounds of reverie.

(almost imperceptibly, lights pick up Victor and the Creature)

I saw—with shut eyes but acute mental vision—I saw the pale student of unhallowed arts kneeling beside the thing he had put together. I saw the hideous phantasm of a man stretched out ... the horrid thing looking on him with yellow, watery, but speculative eyes.

BYRON: You look as if you've been wrestling with the angel.

MARY: I think—I think I've got a story.

BYRON: I'm envious.

MARY: A fluke—a transcript of the grim terrors of my waking dream. . . .

BYRON: What luck! Ridiculous, really. Shelley's paramour, inamorata, dare I say it: whore. Whore, except that she was also the daughter of that banshee in skirts and female liberationist, Mrs. Wollstonecraft, going on about the rights of women—education, sexual freedom, what-have-you. So: not whore but free woman, new woman, only sixteen, girl, really. But we! We—incipient geniuses! We were the writers! The challenge was a ghost story, and she beat us hands down! Ludicrous. And—just.

15

GODWIN: Stick to the rigor of the novel, Mary. Only lazy persons write for the theatre.

MARY: Yes, Papa.

GODWIN: The scope and complexity of the novel requires hundreds of pages, each crammed with words. Beside it, a play is merely a sketch, every page hardly marked with ink. And the novel conveys far more vigorously than any tract the wreckage of social injustice, except for your mother's tracts. They surpassed her novels, oddly enough, and proved vastly more influential.

MARY: Byron wanted—

GODWIN: But no plays!

MARY: A novel, Papa. A ghost story.

GODWIN: It's in your blood. From my side, my dear. *Caleb Williams, St. Leon, Fleetwood.*

BYRON: No one reads them.

GODWIN: Everyone prefers my political philosophy.

BYRON: "Prefer" is a bit rich.

GODWIN: My *Enquiry Concerning Political Justice.*

BYRON: Exhaustive, voluminous, extended, not to say endless inquiry.

MARY: You expect me to take up my mother's cause. But I am more partial to my father's inquiry. And even now, in my waning years, I keep . . . wondering if justice is possible, and if so, what are its essentials. But no matter. We are aiming for a ghost story. . . . *(lighting a candle, or oil lamp)* Once again, my dear but hideous progeny, go forth! Work your spell! Prosper!

VICTOR: I beg your pardon, but I believe this is my story.

MARY: Yes, of course, yours, Victor Frankenstein's.

VICTOR: I tell the tale.

MARY: You among others.

VICTOR: But I am the central figure. Except for . . . my own progeny. Which, by definition, I myself bring forth.

MARY: As I you.

VICTOR: Shall I thank you?

MARY: We digress. Captain Walton tells of you telling your tale, which includes allowing the Creature to tell its tale—

VICTOR: A fatal flaw.

BYRON: Pure genius.

MARY: One inside the other, each a different—

VICTOR: Creation.

MARY: Indeed.

VICTOR: Mine.

MARY: Yes, yes, let's not be silly. My story is your story.

VICTOR: Your story is my story.

MARY: Oh, do tell it, please.

VICTOR: When I tell it, I live it. It's . . . difficult.

MARY: For me too, yes, I understand.

VICTOR: Then why?

MARY: To warn the reader.

VICTOR: Of?

MARY: You don't know?

VICTOR: They've been warned and warned. What's the good?

MARY: The next time it may stick.

VICTOR: Why bother? Show them what must be done!

MARY: If you would begin.

VICTOR: Please.

MARY: Either version, the beginning's the same, isn't it?

VICTOR: You'll allow me to—?

MARY: You were a child of loving . . .

VICTOR: *(simultaneous)* I was the child of loving parents, who pitied my innocence and helplessness, and brought me up to be good. When I was about five, they adopted a lovely orphan, Elizabeth, who became my more than sister, mine to protect, love, and cherish.

(discover Elizabeth at her needlework, then fading out)

MARY: Elizabeth pored over her needlework and contemplated appearances while Victor studied causes, zealous to fathom the secrets of heaven and earth.

VICTOR: An empty vessel, longing to be filled to the brim!

MARY: *(overlapping)* Their friend, Henry Clerval, occupied himself with the moral relations of things.

(Henry in his study fades in and out)

VICTOR: Idyllic childhood! Later misfortune hewed my destiny.

MARY: Natural philosophy regulated your days.

(Victor picks up a book, begins to leaf through it, becomes increasingly absorbed in it)

At thirteen you chanced upon a volume of Cornelius Agrippa.

(discover Alphonse)

VICTOR: Father!

ALPHONSE: My dear Victor, do not waste your time. Cornelius Agrippa is sad trash. *(fades out)*

VICTOR: *(calling)* You barely glanced at it! *(to himself)* Has he read it?

(Mary, Henry, and Alphonse appear with short stacks of books. Some volumes they place on the study table, some they hand directly to Victor. Captain Walton follows them but remains apart at his own desk, setting out his writing materials, recording the story as it unfolds.)

I read avidly—

MARY: Agrippa.

HENRY: Paracelsus.

ALPHONSE: Albertus Magnus—now there's a thinker!

CAPTAIN WALTON: I much prefer Isaac Newton—picking up shells beside the great and unexplored ocean of truth.

MARY: His successors embrace the same pursuit, partially unveiling the face of Nature—yet her immortal lineaments are still a wonder and a mystery.

VICTOR: The men my father scorns will help me storm the citadel of nature. I am enthralled! *(to Mary)* Must I say that?

MARY: It's there.

VICTOR: "Enthralled"? With Newton?

MARY: The diction suits a ghost story.

VICTOR: But if we are showing what must be done—

MARY: For now—

VICTOR: We should mention—

MARY: Let's go on.

(Victor pores over his texts as the others continue to pile books around him, nearly blocking him from view)

ALPHONSE: If you insist on doing it—

VICTOR: She insists, not I!

ALPHONSE: Then do it thoroughly, completely!

HENRY: With the greatest diligence!

CAPTAIN WALTON: In search of the philosopher's stone—the elixir of life!

HENRY: You don't think you may be overdoing it?

VICTOR: How can one overdo the search for truth?

HENRY: Ever hear of a fellow named Faust?

VICTOR: I am not amused, Henry. Faust has nothing to do with it. He sold his soul—I'm just working hard. *(to Mary)* Let's get on with it!

MARY: Exactly.

VICTOR: This is the point. Once we've made it, what's left?

MARY: One point of many—please continue.

VICTOR: How many points?

MARY: Immaterial.

VICTOR: Since you force me to continue, please do me the courtesy.

MARY: Your unquenchable curiosity!

VICTOR: A simple question.

MARY: I have not counted my points. That's an enterprise more suited to serious debate than to frivolous pastimes. But I do know that I have more than this one. Henry, please.

HENRY: Faust wanted to know everything—just like you.

VICTOR: Henry! Have a little gumption! Am I telling her story? Or is she telling mine?

HENRY: She is the author.

VICTOR: So I must mouth banalities? Reduce what I suffered to the imaginings of a sixteen-year-old child?

MARY: Only a way to while away an evening. And my adolescent imagination floats unshackled, free of the constraints of experience.

VICTOR: Have you never thirsted for a means to improve our human lot? Have you never found yourself nearly crushed by your creation's force? The creation assumes its own contour.

MARY: Please just go on.

VICTOR: The creation spurs possibilities you cannot foresee. It exercises influence of questionable morality. And you, its creator, recalling your original impulse—

MARY: It's only a ghost story!

VICTOR: Stop saying that! The intentions behind your original impulse have evaporated—and you are left with—thin air.

MARY: In any case, you are telling your story to him. *(turning to Captain Walton, who is still taking notes)* And he will tell it to the world.

VICTOR: A mere device. What matters here are noble intentions gone wrong! And the impossibility of making them go right!

HENRY: *(getting back to his script)* Faust wanted to know everything, just—

VICTOR: I want to help humanity! What glory to banish disease from the human frame and render man invulnerable to any but a violent death!

HENRY: Dream on, Victor—but don't let these fancies carry you off.

VICTOR: Other visions, too—my authors promise the raising of ghosts. *(to Mary)* Since I lack piety, I do not subscribe to resurrection.

HENRY: Now there I draw the line!

MARY: The raising of ghosts poses an essential question.

VICTOR: Let them lie! Let them return to the earth! We must face the present and confront the monsters lurking in the shadows of our own hopes!

HENRY: Physician, heal thyself.

VICTOR: I am doing my utmost! I've failed so far—a fault in the pupil, not the instructors. But I can't give up, Henry—not until I've exhausted all the possibilities!

CAPTAIN WALTON: You'll exhaust yourself first, my friend. Please. Be sensible.

(Victor sits, spent. Sounds of storm; lightning flashes. Montage of images: Einstein's face, a mushroom cloud, Three-Mile Island, cloned sheep. He jumps up. Another flash.)

VICTOR: Electricity and galvanism incinerate Cornelius Agrippa, Paracelsus, and Albertus Magnus. Can I ever catch up with what is known? Let alone hack a new trail through the wilderness of ignorance?

(Returning the books to Mary, who hands them off to their various distributors)

Pseudo-knowledge! Only mathematics is reliable! . . . This almost miraculous change of inclination and will was the immediate suggestion of the guardian angel of my life—the last effort to avert the storm even then hanging in the stars ready to envelop me.

CAPTAIN WALTON: Destiny's immutable laws had decreed—

VICTOR: My utter and terrible destruction.

MARY: At seventeen, Victor was about to depart for the university of Ingolstadt when Elizabeth caught scarlet fever. Despite the family's entreaties to refrain from nursing her, Victor's mother, as old then as I am now, attended her ward.

(Lights pick up a figure, Caroline, swathed in a dress. As she topples over backward onto a chaise longue, Elizabeth crawls out from underneath the dress.)

VICTOR: Elizabeth is saved!

23

MARY: But her preserver suffered fatal consequences.

(Justine ministers to Caroline through what follows. Alphonse stands nearby)

VICTOR: *(taking Elizabeth's hand, escorting her toward Caroline)* On her deathbed, she joined Elizabeth's hands with mine.

CAROLINE: My firmest hopes of future happiness rely on the prospect of your union. This expectation will now be the consolation of your father.

ALPHONSE: Please, Caroline—

CAROLINE: Do not humor me, Alphonse. Elizabeth, my love, you must supply my place to my younger children.

VICTOR: Bit of a stretch.

ALPHONSE: Caroline!

CAROLINE: I have been blessed, I have been fortunate. But now I am not so sure. You are so dear, so precious, each of you surpassing in your person the wealth of the richest sultan or king! I cannot quit you all! I cannot!

ELIZABETH: Madame Frankenstein, please, please be calm. You gave everything to nurse me through the fever. Please, please! Let God spare her life!

VICTOR: Mamma!

(Lights pick up Godwin and Mary Wollstonecraft's portrait projected)

MARY: Mamma!

GODWIN: There was no retaining her. Your birth cost her life.

MARY: I am doing my utmost to make up for that, Papa.

GODWIN: No retrieving her.

MARY: She is not dead, she is only sleeping.

GODWIN: We did everything even remotely useful.

CAROLINE: I must resign myself—

VICTOR: No! *(moaning under)*

GODWIN: She slipped away. And you, Mary . . .

VICTOR: No, no, no, please, no . . .

GODWIN: You must take her place . . .

CAROLINE: Resign myself cheerfully . . .

MARY: I'll try, Papa.

CAROLINE: . . . to death.

GODWIN: She casts a long shadow.

CAROLINE: *(caressing Victor)* But I cannot! Dearest Victor! I will not see you fulfill your bright promise!

ALPHONSE: We shall reunite in another world.

CAROLINE: Oh, Alphonse! Leave off your false comforts!

ALPHONSE: It's true!

CAROLINE: I don't care! I want to stay! Here! Now! Justine!

JUSTINE: Madame.

CAROLINE: Where are you?

JUSTINE: *(taking her hand)* Here, Madame.

VICTOR AND MARY: Mother!

25

GODWIN: A great woman of compassion and determination.

ELIZABETH: Come, Victor. Please.

GODWIN: Her work will live for generations. And who knows?

ELIZABETH: We must go on.

GODWIN: Perhaps in some small way—your own way, I should say—we all have a place.

ELIZABETH: We are left here . . .

GODWIN: *(leaving)* And I must get to mine.

ELIZABETH: We must continue.

(Elizabeth exits. Mary and Victor go to Caroline as the lights crossfade to Henry.)

HENRY: I thought my father would come 'round if I—subsided—for a while. Old fellow never succumbs to battering. Even after various proddings and pleadings, well—

VICTOR: *(entering)* Persuade him!

HENRY: He refuses.

VICTOR: I'll see to it.

HENRY: He won't budge.

VICTOR: Your father is a narrow-minded trader.

HENRY: He has my welfare at heart.

VICTOR: He has no soul!

HENRY: University means idleness and ruin. *(with a shrug)* Well—my misfortune. I am yet resolved to slip the chains of commerce. And if only one of us can go to university, better you than I.

VICTOR: He refuses, I refuse.

HENRY: You must go.

VICTOR: I won't!

HENRY: You must.

VICTOR: Only if you do.

HENRY: I can't. And you must. It's what you are meant to do and to be.

(They embrace, and Henry fades. "Gaudeamus igitur" under, as lights pick up Professor Krempe reviewing Victor's dossier.)

VICTOR: I am starved for knowledge.

PROFESSOR KREMPE: So I see.

VICTOR: Until now, my only teachers have been—

PROFESSOR KREMPE: Alchemists.

VICTOR: Well, partly.

PROFESSOR KREMPE: Alchemists? Have you really spent your time on such nonsense?

VICTOR: Why, yes, I—

PROFESSOR KREMPE: Mr. Frankenstein—if this is your idea of an amusing prank, it's a prank gone awry.

VICTOR: No, sir, really—I assure you—they have inspired me! Not lead into gold—

PROFESSOR KREMPE: I should hope not.

VICTOR: But—the source of life! The secret of the soul!

PROFESSOR KREMPE: *(disdainfully)* That.

VICTOR: If we can penetrate these mysteries—

PROFESSOR KREMPE: I'm not so sure we want to go down that road.

VICTOR: We can conquer disease and even—even death!

PROFESSOR KREMPE: And I know we don't want to go down that one.

VICTOR: Because you condemn the alchemists. Even if their methods—

PROFESSOR KREMPE: Methods! Every instant you have wasted on those books is utterly and entirely lost. You have burdened your memory with exploded systems and useless names. Good God! In what desert land have you lived, where no one was kind enough to inform you that these fancies . . . are a thousand years old and as musty as they are ancient? A disciple of Albertus Magnus and Paracelsus! Who knows what harm these pursuits have inflicted on your ability to pursue modern thinking?

VICTOR: I'll learn, sir! I'll unlearn the old, and I'll—

PROFESSOR KREMPE: My dear fellow, you must sweep out all those antiquated furnishings in your brain and start from the beginning. There's hardly time.

VICTOR: I am determined, sir.

PROFESSOR KREMPE: Oh, are you now?

VICTOR: I plan to devote myself to—

PROFESSOR KREMPE: Oh, do you now? *(leaving)*

VICTOR: *(calling after him)* I won't rest until I—

PROFESSOR KREMPE: *(nearly off)* Oh, won't you now? They all say that when they arrive, you know.

Somehow you never hear another word about it. And when they leave . . . when they leave . . .

(discover Professor Waldman, a kindly, modest fellow, lecturing informally)

PROFESSOR WALDMAN: The ancient teachers of this science promised everything and performed nothing. The modern masters are a bit more modest. They promise very little. They know that metals cannot be transmuted. They are certain that the elixir of life is a chimera. But these moderns, whose hands dabble in dirt, and whose eyes pore over the microscopic evidence, the residue in the crucible, have indeed performed miracles. They penetrate into the recesses of nature and show how she works in her hiding places. They ascend into the heavens: they have discovered how the blood circulates, and the nature of the air we breathe. They have acquired new and almost unlimited powers; they can command the thunders of heaven, mimic the earthquake, and even mock the invisible world with its own shadows. So much has been done. Yet much remains.

VICTOR: More, far more, will I achieve: . . . pioneer a new way, explore unknown powers, and unfold to the world the deepest mysteries of creation.

PROFESSOR WALDMAN: Ah, yes, Cornelius Agrippa, Paracelsus. They have their place, bringing to light certain facts for us to arrange in connected classifications. The labors of men of genius, however erroneously directed, ultimately turn to the advantage of humanity.

VICTOR: But listening to you, sir—I too want to fathom nature's depths.

29

PROFESSOR WALDMAN: Well, now—you needn't go that far.

VICTOR: Oh, but I do—I want to go to the ends of the earth—where no one has got to before, sir. Oh, think of it! To discover the secrets of life, to decipher the enigma of the universe! I snatch at a thread of hope, praying for the time and the inspiration to weave a little patch of the evolving fabric of human progress. I don't sign my name, but I do leave the faintest trace along the trail of our common struggle.

PROFESSOR WALDMAN: Yes . . . well . . . callow youth.

VICTOR: Scorn me, scorn my—

PROFESSOR WALDMAN: Rampant enthusiasm.

VICTOR: I'll settle into a more measured demeanor all too soon. But, please, Professor Waldman—do not dismiss me because I nurse a spark of idealism.

PROFESSOR WALDMAN: Time will extinguish that spark.

VICTOR: As it has yours?

PROFESSOR WALDMAN: Impertinence.

VICTOR: Why discourage me?

PROFESSOR WALDMAN: I want to save you dashing down a cul-de-sac.

VICTOR: Science expects dead ends. I'll tunnel to the side.

PROFESSOR WALDMAN: We won't explore those we have already mapped.

VICTOR: I know I'm just starting out, sir, but—

PROFESSOR WALDMAN: If you want to become a man of science, however, and not merely a petty experimentalist, apply to every branch of natural philosophy, including mathematics. *(exits)*

(Gradually, almost imperceptibly, a mound of clothes and a pile of mannekins and their parts emerges. Faint music fades in and continues under.)

VICTOR: Whence . . . does the principle of life proceed? . . . Anatomy is not sufficient; I must also observe the natural decay of the human body. . . . *(moving toward the heap of mannekins)* Can the corruption of death succeed to the blooming cheek of life? Once the worm inherits the wonders of the eye and brain, can we reverse the cycle? After days and nights of incredible labor and fatigue, I succeeded in discovering the cause of generation and life; nay, more, I became myself capable of bestowing animation upon lifeless matter.

BYRON: *(dangling a handful of vermicelli)* Ecco!

VICTOR: And if that, I might in process of time . . . renew life where death had apparently devoted the body to corruption.

(Some of the mannekins' parts, along with an occasional skirt, shirt, tunic or dress, begin slowly to rise to suggest partially formed figures. As these multiply, the shadows disperse. Working various pulleys, Victor sorts and selects and tries various combinations.)

BYRON: *(turning to Mary)* Really! Preposterous! Inspired! I am going over to the animists!

MARY: He collected bones from charnel houses and disturbed, with profane fingers, the tremendous secrets of the human frame.

BYRON: Oh, that's good—grisly, scientific, and illegal all in one!

31

MARY: The dissecting room and the slaughterhouse furnished his materials as he devoted heart and soul to this one pursuit.

PROFESSOR WALDMAN: Is that possible? The laws of nature forbid it!

MARY: I imagine, I speculate. Some day the laws of science may penetrate the secret. It is clumsy, tracing patterns, stitching bits together like a patchwork quilter. Like a surgeon.

(lights discover Alphonse at his hearth, with Elizabeth nearby engaged in needlework)

ALPHONSE: . . . while you are pleased with yourself— and with good cause, we all rejoice in your achievements—think of us with affection, and write regularly. If you let your correspondence lapse, I'll take it that your other duties are equally neglected.

VICTOR: I am a student, I must pursue my studies. Allow me that, Father. Exceptional pursuits prevent tranquil domestic affections. Otherwise . . .

MARY: Greece had not been enslaved; Caesar would have spared his country; and the empires of Mexico and Peru had not been destroyed.

(Moonlight. Steady rain falling. Victor, exhausted, throws himself onto a chaise. Flickering candlelight makes the scene shimmer. Music increasingly strange, resembling the sounds of an intensive-care unit—periodic, percussive. After a few moments the Creature opens an eye. Victor freezes, unsure of what he has seen. His actions seem to mimic unwittingly those of his creation. Pause. The Creature blinks, convulses, jerks up. Victor bounds to his feet. As the Creature comes alive, Victor moves away yet remains fixed on his creation.)

VICTOR: This is a dream, a dream! Let me sleep on! Let me savor this amazement and delight! Soon I will awaken and you will disappear! Please, please do not vanish!

(the Creature turns toward him)

It moves! It moves! The gods have blessed my endeavor! And here before me, in my waking life, I contemplate my destiny fulfilled!

(at first the effect is of a beautiful awakening: as Victor describes it, the attractive features emerge first, the grotesque registering only afterward)

Oh! Is it possible? *(awed)* His limbs are in proportion, his features beautiful. . . . *(approaching the Creature)* Great God! His yellow skin scarcely covers the muscles and arteries; yet his flowing hair is black, lustrous; his teeth of pearly whiteness. Horrid contrast to his watery eyes, almost the color of their dun-white sockets, his shriveled complexion, his straight black lips! Destiny as catastrophe! *(turns away in horror)*

(Discover Elizabeth setting aside her needlework. Victor sees her, doubts his eyes, then embraces her.)

Elizabeth! You here! Not a dream! Oh, my dearest love!

(As he kisses her, she turns a frightening, masked face toward him. Twisting, writhing, both in his dream and watching it, Victor grasps a throw from the chaise, clutches it to his chest, and cries out.)

Mother!

(The figure in the dress topples over. A newborn baby cries.)

33

I held her corpse in my arms, shrouded, grave worms crawling in the folds of flannel. *(Flings fabric away. Looking up at the curtained casement, cries out.)* Miserable wretch! My God! What have I done?

(Creature tries to speak, managing some nonverbal sounds. Slowly it smiles and tentatively extends its hand. Victor cries out and rushes away. Blackout.)

Scene 2

Dawn light gradually intensifying as the clock strikes six times. Rain lashes against the eaves, developing into a steady downpour. Thunder and lightning.

VICTOR: *(shivering with anxiety)* Such a thing even Dante did not conceive!

"Like one, that on a lonesome road,
Doth walk in fear and dread,
And having once turned round walks on,
And turns no more his head;
Because he knows, a frightful fiend
Doth close behind him tread."

A being of such ugliness! *(to Mary)* I must be allowed the chance to set things right!

CAPTAIN WALTON: He has a point.

MARY: We'll see.

(Henry enters, carrying a valise. Not recognizing him, Victor starts.)

HENRY: Victor? Don't you—?

VICTOR: Henry Clerval!

HENRY: My dear Frankenstein, how glad I am to see you! The instant of my alighting!

VICTOR: My dear Henry! I too am filled with joy at seeing you! Your father has clearly relented!

HENRY: Only by dint of my near heroic efforts! I had to persuade him that some vital knowledge existed outside the noble art of bookkeeping. He kept arguing like the Dutch schoolmaster in *The Vicar of Wakefield*: "I have ten thousand florins a year without Greek, I eat heartily without Greek; and, in short, as I don't know Greek, there is no good in it." Luckily, his love for me surpasses his contempt for learning. Thus he has finally capitulated and financed my voyage of discovery to the land of knowledge.

VICTOR: Oh! How providential!

HENRY: I am graced, blessed, one of the elect!

VICTOR: And I too in your presence! Oh! Quick, tell me all the news! How is my father? My brother? Elizabeth?

HENRY: Very well, very happy. *(after hesitating)* A little uneasy hearing from you so seldom.

VICTOR: Something has happened.

HENRY: No, no, but . . . my dear Frankenstein—I hardly know you! You are ill—gaunt and pale, as if you haven't slept for several nights.

VICTOR: You see right through me, Henry. I am exhausted to the marrow. But I have finished my work—I am free.

(as lights pick up casement, Victor recoils, afraid to look)

HENRY: Then my arrival is most opportune! We'll have a deserved holiday!

(Victor gathers courage and turns)

VICTOR: *(crying out in relief)* Ah! Empty.

HENRY: I beg your pardon?

VICTOR: *(clapping his hands joyfully)* I am free! *(nearing hysterics)* Like a hawk gliding! *("flying" about)*

HENRY: My dear Victor!

VICTOR: We must uncover the aerodynamical principle of avian flight. Have you studied Leonardo's notebooks? I shall engineer the wings while you recite lofty . . . soaring . . . verse! *(manic)* Free! Free!

HENRY: What, for God's sake, is the matter?

VICTOR: *(coming to an abrupt halt)* I thought—I dreamed—something . . . unspeakable! I awoke and was unsure. But it was a dream! It was a dream! It was!

HENRY: How ill you are!

VICTOR: If I could tell you, I would, but—oh! We are at risk! He'll know where we—don't ask! Oh, save me! Save me! *(clinging to Henry)* Somehow—there will be a way, we must think of a way to—oh!

HENRY: Victor! Wait! Here. Sit. Calm yourself!

(Henry helps him to a chair)

VICTOR: Dearest Henry, how kind, how very good you are to me.

HENRY: What are friends for?

VICTOR: How shall I ever repay you?

HENRY: Get well as fast as you can. And . . . I may speak on one subject, may I not?

VICTOR: *(with a start)* What?

HENRY: Please, Victor, compose yourself. Your father and cousin Elizabeth would delight to have a letter from you in your own handwriting. They have no idea how ill you are, but, nevertheless, they are uneasy at your long silence.

VICTOR: Is that all? My first thought flies to those dear, dear friends who are so deserving of my love.

HENRY: Then you will be glad to see this letter from your cousin.

(as Victor takes the letter, light comes up on Elizabeth)

VICTOR: My dearest cousin, you have been ill, . . .

ELIZABETH: . . . forbidden to hold a pen; yet one word from you, dear Victor, to calm our apprehensions. Return to us and a happy, cheerful home. Your father's health is vigorous, and how pleased you would be to see little darling William! Tall, with sweet laughing blue eyes, dark eyelashes, curling hair.

(reverberating child's laughter)

Since you left us, but one change has taken place in our little household. Do you remember Justine Moritz?

VICTOR: Of course! She came to live in our house when her father died—her mother could not endure her.

ELIZABETH: She adored your mother and thought her the model of all excellence. When she died, Justine was very ill, but other trials were reserved for

37

her. Her brothers and sister died. Her mother, now childless except for Justine, began to think on her sorrows as judgment, and called Justine home. Oh, how Justine wept at leaving us! Nor did residing again with her mother restore her to gaiety, for sometimes Madame Moritz begged Justine to forgive her unkindness, and sometimes blamed her for having caused the deaths of her brothers and sister. Now Madame Moritz is at peace forever, and Justine has returned to us, very clever and gentle and extremely pretty. Otherwise we go on as we were when you last came home. . . . Write, dearest Victor—one line—one word will be a blessing to us.

(lights out on Elizabeth)

VICTOR: Dear, dear Elizabeth! I will write at once, Henry—and then you must meet my professors— who will soon be yours!

(Henry begins to set out writing materials)

PROFESSOR WALDMAN: *(entering)* Ah! Frankenstein! I must congratulate you on your recovery! We are in your debt, Mr. Clerval. But what is your health compared to your work? Mere bagatelle. Tuppence. Trifle.

HENRY: If he does not fully recover, he cannot resume his work.

VICTOR: My work! Ah! Yes, yes of course, thank you.

PROFESSOR WALDMAN: The strides you have taken in your studies!

VICTOR: Please, sir. . . .

PROFESSOR WALDMAN: Modest as ever, I see. Well—you needn't be our subject. Natural philosophy itself—

VICTOR: Please, sir.

HENRY: My friend demurs on my behalf, Professor Waldman. Victor knows I know nothing of such studies. Of course, you might speak of natural philosophy, and I of Sanskrit studies, so that we would both feel equally left out.

PROFESSOR WALDMAN: You have me there.

HENRY: On the other hand, we might talk more generally—of letters, say, or . . .

PROFESSOR KREMPE: *(entering)* Damn the fellow's modesty, Mr. Clerval. Why, he has outstripped us all! Oh, stare if you please—it's true! He arrived a devotée of Cornelius Agrippa, mind you! *(laughing)* Agrippa was gospel! And now he's at the top of the university! Oh, it's all very fine when you're young. I myself was well known in my youth for my modesty, when there seemed plenty of time for deserved recognition. But in one's twilight years, time races along, and modesty subsides.

HENRY: As in your case, sir, or so I understand from my friend, it should.

PROFESSOR KREMPE: Nicely put, Mr. Clerval. I thank you for the sentiment. We do not strut, we do not. But on occasion, a little basking never harmed anyone. *(wandering off with Professor Waldman)* Why, when I came to Ingolstadt in . . .

HENRY: Must one overlook self-deception in one's elders?

VICTOR: It's the wiser course.

HENRY: He was born with a strut.

BYRON: I was born with a twisted foot.

MARY: This isn't about you.

BYRON: Of course it isn't, I didn't write it. *Don Juan* is about me. *Childe Harold* is about me. But *Frankenstein!* My dear. Do allow me some shred of acuity.

HENRY: *(to Victor)* I have a prescription. We shall attack Sanskrit together—you will find its melancholy soothing.

VICTOR: Excellent friend! How sincerely you love me and endeavor to elevate my mind to the level of your own! But more melancholy may prove too much.

HENRY: Such a dunce, Victor! You need reminding of life's joys.

VICTOR: I've been too much alone, Henry. With you here, I realize how much I've lacked your company.

HENRY: My joy is in yours. I shall lock up the Sanskrit.

VICTOR: No need, since I cannot read it.

HENRY: Its melancholy is sealed—harmless Sanskrit!

VICTOR: Would science were like it in its benevolence!

HENRY: Only your ignorance of Sanskrit makes you deaf to its siren song, Victor. Only my ignorance of science allows me to plead innocent of its—

VICTOR: Do not remind me!

HENRY: Please, Victor, be calm.

VICTOR: Yes, yes, I will be. And upon that calm I'll sow a garden of courage to border a fortress of optimism. And I will hoist the banner of hope!

BYRON: *(to Mary)* A trifle florid, don't you know.

(lights discover Alphonse as Victor picks up the letter)

ALPHONSE: How shall I inflict pain on my long-absent son? Even now your eye skims over the page, to seek the words. . . .

VICTOR: William is dead!

ALPHONSE: Sweet child, whose smiles delighted and warmed my heart, who was so gentle. . . ! Victor, he is—

VICTOR: Murdered!

(Happy shrieks, laughter, of boys playing. Elizabeth voiceover—"Don't go too far!" More laughing, continuing under.)

ALPHONSE: Last Thursday I went to walk with Elizabeth and your brother. As usual, he dallied behind and dashed ahead, so that we thought nothing of his periodic disappearances. At dusk, however, William was not to be found.

(Elizabeth voiceover—"William! William! Come out now! It's time to go home!")

ALPHONSE: Alarmed, we searched till night fell, then returned to the house, expecting—hoping, rather—to find him curled up on the window seat, or cradling the cat. But he was . . . not there.

(A sweep of light. Elizabeth enters, pushing a gurney with the covered form of the lifeless William.)

I . . . we returned to the woods with torches, and . . . about five in the morning . . . discovered my lovely boy. *(going to the gurney, he turns back the covering)* My dearest child! *(getting control of himself)* The night before, apple-cheeked, dashing into the woods, but now . . . stretched out on the grass, livid and deathly still: the print of the murderer's finger was on his neck.

ELIZABETH: Oh God! I have murdered my darling child!

VICTOR: Elizabeth?! What are you saying?!

ALPHONSE: Elizabeth had let William wear a valuable miniature of your mother.

(Caroline's and Mary Wollstonecraft's images projected)

ELIZABETH: As a comfort. He begged me—he was distraught over a dream. He awoke thinking her death was a dream, expecting her to appear as usual on the threshold of his room. Then he realized the dream was false and her death the truth, and he was beside himself. So I . . . and now! If only I had—!

ALPHONSE: This picture is gone and was doubtless the murderer's temptation. . . . Our exertions to discover him are unremitting; but they will not restore my beloved William! Your dear mother! Thank God she did not live to witness this cruel, miserable death of her youngest darling!

(Elizabeth exits with William. Victor hands Henry the letter.)

HENRY: My dear Frankenstein! Your disaster is irreparable.

VICTOR: I must go instantly to Geneva.

HENRY: I'll go with you.

VICTOR: No, no. I must face this alone.

HENRY: Please, Victor, let me accompany you. You're already susceptible to—

VICTOR: Please. Allow me my grief.

HENRY: Poor William! He now sleeps with his angel mother. You're sure you—

VICTOR: Absolutely.

HENRY: How much more monstrous the murderer, to destroy such radiant innocence! One consolation—he is at rest.

VICTOR: If that were true!

HENRY: What else? William was pure—

VICTOR: William. Of course.

HENRY: Farewell, dear friend. *(embracing him)* And Godspeed.

VICTOR: On my journey home, a thousand nameless evils overcame me. By degrees, calm and the heavenly scene restored me. So vast and awesome, it restored my sense of my own limits. The black sides of Jura and the bright summit of Mont Blanc. Dear mountains! My own beautiful lake! How do you welcome your wanderer! Is this to prognosticate peace or to mock at my unhappiness?

(sound and light effects of thunderstorm continuing under)

The lake! A vast sheet of fire! William! Dear angel! This is thy funeral and dirge!

(The Creature appears in the shadows. Victor cries out. The Creature disappears.)

My first thought—I must tell what I know of the murderer.

MARY: Oh?

VICTOR: Yes, of course—what else?

BYRON: Better to commandeer a post chaise and ride hell-for-leather to the ends of the earth.

VICTOR: I am not so impulsive. I work within the boundaries of prudence.

BYRON: Ah.

VICTOR: But how to tell my story?

MARY: Mine.

BYRON: Some say Shelley's.

MARY: You well know the truth of that scurrility.

VICTOR: A being whom I myself had formed—

MARY: *(overlapping)* There's the rub.

VICTOR:—my nervous fever—I still sometimes spoke incoherently, full of stops and starts, thought tumbling and jumbling, or—only half-formed notions, each being interrupted with some other—if another had told me such stuff I should have looked upon it as the ravings of insanity. In fact, if I listened to myself, I would agree. How might I expect otherwise?

BYRON: You expect to persuade us?

VICTOR: I expect nothing.

BYRON: Hope, then.

VICTOR: Nor do I hope. I simply report my—condition.

BYRON: *(to Mary)* A bit feeble, you must admit.

VICTOR: I admit nothing!

BYRON: My dear fellow! I am your elder in mischief as in years. Kindly refrain from addressing me unless I have first—

VICTOR: I am merely playing out the destiny she has decreed!

BYRON: No gumption.

VICTOR: How else may I choose?

BYRON: You've definitely rejected the post chaise? At least one other course springs to mind.

MARY: *(to Victor)* Ignore him.

VICTOR: I need to know.

BYRON: That insatiable curiosity again! *(to Mary)* Is he a bounder?

MARY: He is deeply frightened. His thoughts are fragmented. Voices jangle in his head. He has not foreseen the implications—

BYRON: That explains it then.

VICTOR: But what—?

BYRON: Nothing, nothing. I spoke out of turn. I have misread your character.

VICTOR: Is that an apology?

BYRON: If you like.

MARY: Please—continue.

VICTOR: Besides . . . even if I had the resources at my disposal to—he would evade pursuit . . . of what use would be pursuit? . . . a creature capable of scaling Mont Salève?

(silence)

I must hold my peace.

BYRON: Ah. *(singing)* "Hold thy peace, and I prithee hold thy peace." I prefer to have another hold my piece. Almost any other.

VICTOR: You are in the presence of a lady.

BYRON: *(looking around)* You are not referring to the daughter of the hyena in petticoats I trust.

VICTOR: Must I remain silent?

MARY: For now.

BYRON: One can always revise.

VICTOR: Later. Later I can come forward—can't I?

BYRON: I should think so.

MARY: It is possible.

BYRON: Although sometimes—when one's character is fully formed—

MARY: He is still evolving.

VICTOR: Not that you would know anything about character.

BYRON: Oh, dear, oh, dear! *(to Mary)* Even if he isn't fully formed, one cannot always turn back.

(discover Alphonse)

VICTOR: Father!

(they embrace)

ALPHONSE: If you had come three months ago! Then we were all joyous and delighted. But now! Now Elizabeth torments herself. She most of all requires consolation. But since the murderer has been discovered—

VICTOR: Good God! Who—how—impossible; one might as well try to overtake the winds, or confine a mountain stream with straw.

ALPHONSE: What are you saying?

VICTOR: The murderer was free last night!

ALPHONSE: I do not know what you mean.

VICTOR: Nor I, nor I—I am not myself.

ALPHONSE: I supposed I'd feel relief—satisfaction—in apprehending . . . but our discovery only com-

46

pounds our misery. Who can believe it? Even now Elizabeth will not be convinced. Indeed, who can credit that Justine Moritz—

VICTOR: Justine!?

ALPHONSE: Exactly—everyone reacts as you do. So amiable and fond of all the family—so appalling a crime.

VICTOR: No one believes it, surely.

ALPHONSE: Circumstances and her own behavior add to the facts a weight that leaves no hope for doubt. But she will be tried today, and then you will hear all.

VICTOR: I know the murderer.

ALPHONSE: Better that we didn't. Better be forever ignorant than discover so much depravity and ingratitude—we sheltered her from her harridan of a mother! We thought her an angel in our midst!

VICTOR: My dear father, you are mistaken. Justine— poor, good Justine—must be innocent. She must be!

ALPHONSE: The odds are slim, but I do hope for her acquittal.

VICTOR: *(almost to himself)* As do we all surely! Madness!

ALPHONSE: The only explanation. We all know madness can strike anyone, poor girl.

VICTOR: If I—no one will believe. . . . If he is let loose upon the world, what will—

ELIZABETH: *(running in)* Cousin! *(taking his hands)* Alas! Who is safe if Justine is convicted?

VICTOR: She cannot be!

ELIZABETH: First, that lovely darling boy; now this poor girl. If she is condemned, I shall grieve forever. But she will not be, she will not, I am sure she will not!

VICTOR: We must look forward to her acquittal.

ELIZABETH: Everyone else believes she is guilty. *(breaking down)* I feel alone, hopeless and despairing.

ALPHONSE: Dearest niece, dry your tears. Rely on the justice of our laws—

ELIZABETH: Oh, Father! I am praying every moment for justice!

ALPHONSE: We are alert to even a shadow of partiality.

(scene gradually shifting to the bars of a prison cell, with Elizabeth gravitating toward Justine)

VICTOR: *(to himself)* A thousand times rather would I have confessed myself guilty . . . but—

(Hubbub of a crowded courtroom, gaveled to silence. Voiceover—"Oyez, Oyez. . . .")

VICTOR: I was absent when it was committed . . . declaration . . . ravings of a madman . . . would not have . . . her who suffered. . . .

JUSTINE: Oh, Mr. Frankenstein! The shame! The shame! When your mother—Madame Frankenstein—

VICTOR: My mother, yes. I miss her.

JUSTINE: I too. At first I was completely at a loss. My own mother had—been indifferent—

VICTOR: She spurned you!

JUSTINE: Yes! Rejected me! And Madame Frankenstein took me to her heart! I was a waif, a stranger

48

at the side of the road, and she offered me refuge and affection. Even more closely did she shelter and comfort me after my own natural mother—

VICTOR: However unnatural.

JUSTINE: After my own finally gave up her soul to its just reward. And then—

VICTOR: Supreme cruelty.

JUSTINE: She herself, nursing Elizabeth, died. And I—and I—I was wild with grief! Torn by—unable to—unable to—Elizabeth herself brought me out of my—my nearly fatal condition—I was the servant, the orphan! Delirium, the doctor said. Hysteria!

VICTOR: Yes, yes, I know, I . . . know.

JUSTINE: They found the picture in my pocket! They found the—! How is it possible?

VICTOR: Certain mental states—one is swept away, not oneself. Not oneself, and so perhaps it is understandable that one cannot remember. . . .

JUSTINE: You think I was transported out of my mind?

VICTOR: I think—I think—other states of consciousness are possible.

JUSTINE: God knows how entirely I am innocent. I hope the character I have always borne will incline my judges to interpret favorably any doubtful or suspicious circumstance.

VICTOR: It will mitigate.

JUSTINE: I had passed a sleepless night looking for William, and was bewildered. The miniature weighs fatally against me, and I cannot explain it. I can only conjecture how it might have been placed in my pocket. But here also I am checked. I

49

believe I have no enemy on earth, and none surely would have been so wicked as to destroy me wantonly. Did the murderer place it there? When? How? And why should he have stolen the jewel, to part with it again so soon? Do you suppose—do you suppose his placing it upon my person was meant as a sign? A message?

VICTOR: What sort of message?

JUSTINE: Oh, I don't know. Somehow, William's murder connects to your mother? Well, of course—he was her child!

VICTOR: *(to himself)* As am I.

JUSTINE: Oh! I am confused, helpless to dispel these shadows!

VICTOR: You must place your trust in the court of justice.

JUSTINE: Oh, I do. I commit my cause to the justice of my judges. Yet I see no room for hope. I beg to have witnesses testify to my character. And if their testimony does not outweigh my supposed guilt, I shall be condemned—although I pledge my salvation on my innocence.

VICTOR: *(to himself)* And if she is not acquitted . . . Oh, God! If I speak, he will know that I know. Please God, her innocence will prevail and give me time to track him.

(Silence. A rustle of movement as the characters take up positions for the trial.)

ELIZABETH: I am the cousin, or rather, sister, of the murdered child, educated by his parents long before his birth. But when I see a fellow creature about to perish through her pretended friends' cowardice, I must say what I know of her character.

(Voiceover—"Murderess! She's a murderess!" Tumult is finally gaveled into murmuring and then silence.)

ELIZABETH: I have lived in the same house with her, at one time for five, and at another for nearly two years, when she appeared the most amiable and benevolent of human creatures. She nursed Madame Frankenstein, my aunt, in her last illness with the greatest affection and care, and afterward attended her own mother during a tedious illness, exciting the admiration of all who knew her. She was attached to William, like an affectionate mother. I believe and rely on her perfect innocence. As to the bauble on which the chief proof rests, if she had asked, I should have willingly given it to her; so much do I esteem and value her. She had no need—she would have had no need—to steal it. *(stepping down)*

(Some reaction from the crowd. Victor breaks away.)

VICTOR: Her innocence will prevail and sustain her.

ELIZABETH: Tell me, Victor.

VICTOR: As you may have expected. All judges had rather ten innocent suffer than one guilty escape. But—you won't believe this—

ELIZABETH: Nothing can surprise me.

VICTOR: She has confessed.

ELIZABETH: No!

VICTOR: I was amazed myself.

BYRON: As well you should be.

ELIZABETH: How shall I ever again trust in human goodness? Justine, whom I loved and esteemed as my sister! *(turning to her)* How can you smile innocently only to betray? You seem so guileless, and yet have committed a murder.

JUSTINE: Let me be!

VICTOR: I must speak.

MARY: Let her be.

VICTOR: *(to Mary)* Give me another choice! Allow me another course!

MARY: You must reject your creation and end in failure.

VICTOR: I am a scientist! I have unleashed a power that exceeds my expectation. I must—rein it in!

MARY: Impossible. Please take your place.

VICTOR: If—if he were welcomed . . .

MARY: Go on.

VICTOR: I—could—recapture his first benign impulses.

MARY: Too late.

ELIZABETH: Oh, Justine! How can you rob me of my last consolation? I was wretched when I relied on your innocence, but now I am in despair.

JUSTINE: As am I!

VICTOR: *(to himself, barely audible)* And I.

(The shadow of the scaffold and its noose appear. The Creature is also dimly perceptible.)

JUSTINE: And do you also believe that I am wicked? Do you also crush and condemn me as a murderer?

ELIZABETH: Why do you kneel if you are innocent? I believed you guiltless, despite every evidence, until I heard you had yourself declared your guilt.

CONFESSOR: How often must I say it? Unless you confess, I cannot grant absolution. You will be cast into eternal fire! Abandon this pretense! Beg for forgiveness! Cast yourself upon God's mercy!

JUSTINE: I confessed a lie. I confessed to obtain absolution, but now that falsehood lies heavier at my heart than all my other sins. The God of heaven forgive me! Ever since I was condemned, you have besieged me.

CONFESSOR: Monster!

JUSTINE: No! I-I-I am dizzy with the unspeakable possibilities! I have lost my way!

VICTOR: A technique. If you had remained steadfast under such an assault—

JUSTINE: He threatened excommunication—

VICTOR: *(overlapping)* But you capitulated.

JUSTINE:—and hellfire in my last moments if I stood my ground. My confessor! How could he mistake?! Who am I, wretched sinner, to gainsay him?! Dear lady, no one supported me. What could I do? In an evil hour I subscribed to a lie, and now I am truly miserable. Lost! Lost! *(breaks down)* Dear William! Dearest blessed child! I soon shall see you again in heaven, where we shall all be happy; and that consoles me as I suffer ignominy and death.

ELIZABETH: Oh, Justine! I am ashamed! Forgive me! Do not mourn, do not fear—I will proclaim, I will prove your innocence. I will melt the frozen hearts of your enemies by my tears and prayers. *(embracing her)* You shall not die! You, my playfellow, my companion, my sister, perish on the scaffold! No! No! I could never survive so horrible a misfortune.

JUSTINE: God raises my weakness and gives me courage to endure the worst. I leave a sad and bitter world. You will remember me?

ELIZABETH: You cannot die.

JUSTINE: And think of me as of one unjustly condemned?

(Elizabeth nods mutely)

I am resigned.

ELIZABETH: You mustn't despair.

JUSTINE: Learn from me, dear lady, to submit in patience to the will of heaven!

VICTOR: *(to himself)* Who dares talk of despair? *(groans)*

JUSTINE: Dear sir, you are very kind to visit me. You, I hope, do not believe that I am guilty?

ELIZABETH: If it were possible, Victor is more convinced of your innocence than I. He does not credit your confession.

JUSTINE: How sweet is your affection! I can die in peace now that you, dear lady, and your cousin affirm my innocence. Please, sir, console yourself. I am at peace.

ELIZABETH: I want to die with you; I cannot live in this world of misery.

JUSTINE: May this be the last misfortune that you will ever suffer! Live, and be happy, and make others so.

(Audio of trap opening, sudden jerk of the noose. Image of Justine hanged. Alphonse enters and embraces Elizabeth.)

VICTOR: You weep, but these are not your last tears! Again you shall raise the funeral wail, and again and again the sound of your lamentations shall be heard!

ALPHONSE: *(to Victor)* No one could love a child more than I loved your brother. But you must not augment our unhappiness by immoderate grief.

ELIZABETH: When I reflect, dear cousin, on Justine's death, I see an alien world. Before I thought vice and injustice imaginary evils; but now misery has come home. Men are monsters thirsting for each other's blood. When falsehood can look so like the truth, who can count on happiness?

ALPHONSE: We must carry on. *(leaves)*

ELIZABETH: William and Justine were assassinated, and their murderer walks free. I would rather suffer on the scaffold for the same crimes than change places with such a wretch. *(leaves)*

VICTOR: Your dear faces mirror my own grief. I, who would spend my life serving you, bid you weep! Shed countless tears, if thus we shall satisfy fate!

ACT 2

Scene 1

Mountains and ice, set off by a whining wind. Victor alone, resting, taking in the scene. The Creature again dimly perceived.

VICTOR: Wandering spirits, if indeed you wander and do not rest in your narrow beds, allow me this faint happiness. If not, take me, as your companion, away from the joys of life.

(lights discover Creature)

Devil! You dare approach me? Oh, that I could extinguish your miserable existence and restore those you have murdered!

CREATURE: How dare you sport thus with life? Do your duty toward me, and I will do mine toward you and the rest of mankind.

VICTOR: Wretched devil! You reproach me with your creation? Then let me extinguish the spark I so negligently ignited!

CREATURE: Be calm. Have I not suffered enough?

VICTOR: What is that to these dear lives lost?

CREATURE: Why increase my misery? I am thy creature, and I will be ever mild and docile to my natural lord and king. But you must do your part.

VICTOR: I have! Would that I had not!

CREATURE: I ought to be your Adam, but I am rather your Lucifer. Make me happy, and I shall again be virtuous. Life, even if it has been only accumulated anguish, is dear to me.

VICTOR: As dear to those whose lives you snatched!

CREATURE: How can I move you? Am I not alone, miserably alone? You, my creator, abhor me; your fellow creatures spurn and hate me. Shall I not hate them who abhor me?

VICTOR: I will not hear you. We are enemies.

CREATURE: Let your compassion be moved, and do not disdain me. The guilty are allowed, bloody as they are, to speak in their own defense before they are condemned. You accuse me of murder, and yet you would destroy your own creature—is that not murder? And did you not stand silent as Justine mounted the gallows?

VICTOR: I expected an acquittal. I did not want to show my hand, so as to pursue you more effectively.

CREATURE: You were terrified.

VICTOR: I was paralyzed by the results of my arrogance!

CREATURE: Arrogance stops your ears. Listen to me, and then, if you can, and if you will, destroy the work of your hands.

VICTOR: I cannot—cannot!—consider if I am just to you. Relieve me! Relieve me from the sight of your detested form!

CREATURE: Thus I relieve you.

57

(He places his hands over Victor's eyes. Victor pulls away with a cry.)

Why did you concoct a thing you find repulsive?

VICTOR: I did not know!! Had I realized the risk, I would have withdrawn my wager!

CREATURE: You would have chosen otherwise? Well! Now I can present you with another choice! You will decide whether I lead a harmless life or terrorize your fellow creatures and speed your ruin.

VICTOR: I am already ruined.

CREATURE: You have made me taller, suppler. Even so, I refuse to attack you.

"Did I request thee, maker, from my clay
To mould me man? Did I solicit thee
From darkness to promote me?"

VICTOR: Please. Spare me. I could not have foreseen my—success.

CREATURE: You refuse to hear my story?

VICTOR: On the contrary. I am desperate for some hint of an explanation.

(reprise of periodic, percussive music from the first scene, and bold contrasts in lighting color what follows)

CREATURE: I am hard pressed to remember my origins—events are confused, blurred. Many sensations seized me—I saw, heard, smelled at the same time—and worked to distinguish one sense from another. Light pressed on my nerves—I had to shut my eyes—darkness then troubled me—then I opened my eyes, light poured in again. Before, dark, opaque bodies, impervious to my touch or sight, had surrounded me; now I wandered at liberty. As the light became increasingly oppressive, and heat fatiguing, I found shade in the forest, ate berries from the trees, drank from a brook, and awoke to cold and desolation. A poor miserable wretch, I sat down and wept.

(moonlight rising)

Then, a radiant form rising from the trees. *(full of wonder)* By its light, I found more berries, and, under a tree, a huge cloak. Days and nights passed, and I learned the stream for drink, the foliage for shade.

(birdsong, which Creature now tries but fails to imitate)

Sometimes I tried to express myself, but my uncouth and inarticulate sounds frightened me into silence. *(demonstrating)* The moon disappeared, then reappeared in a lessened form. I distinguished the insect from the herb, then one herb from another. The sparrow's notes were harsh, but those of the blackbird and the thrush sweet and enticing.

(fire effect)

One day I found an abandoned fire and felt warmth—such delight! I thrust my hand into the embers—ah! One cause, but such opposite effects. I found that the fire was made of wood, and collected some branches. But they were wet and would not burn. Then the wet wood I had placed near the flame dried and flamed. Having discovered this cause, I collected great quantities to dry, so that I might have a plentiful supply. When night came I feared for the fire, and so covered it with dry wood and leaves, and placed wet branches over them. When I uncovered it in the morning, a breeze fanned it into flame, and so I made a fan of branches to rouse the embers when they were nearly extinguished. The fire gave light as well as heat, and so I could search for food. I found the roasted remains of some traveler's meal, and imitated their manner. This spoiled the berries but much improved the nuts and roots.

I had to find food, although I lamented losing my fire, which I did not know how to reproduce. After wandering for three days in a great snowfall, I found a small hut with its door open, an old man preparing his breakfast near the fire. Seeing me

(a shriek)

he sped across the fields. I devoured his breakfast, slept, and set out again, discovering a charming village, with huts, cottages, vegetables in the gardens, milk and cheese at the windows! I had hardly placed my foot upon a threshold when

(Shrieks, stamping of feet, voiceover—"What is it? No, no! Please!" Shrieks, cries, continuing under.)

the whole village was roused—some fled, some attacked me, until, bruised, I took refuge in a bare, low hovel, safe from the inclement season and from such—barbarous men.

My hovel stood adjacent to a cottage, near a clear pool of water. I covered every crevice with stones and wood, carpeted my dwelling with clean straw, and stole a loaf of coarse bread and a cup to drink from the pool. Compared to the bleak forest, this was a paradise. I was safe! Dry, and quiet, and safe!

After breakfast I found a small chink in my dwelling through which I saw a small whitewashed room, bare of furniture. A young man stood by the fire, and a young girl sat down beside an old

man, who took up an instrument—called guitar, I
later learned—and produced sounds sweeter than
the voice of the thrush or the nightingale. A lovely
sight, even to me, especially to me, who had never
beheld anything beautiful before.

(a mournful tune under)

The fair creature sobbed and knelt at his feet.
Then he raised her and smiled with such kindness
and affection that I felt sensations of pain and
pleasure, such as I had never experienced from
hunger or cold, warmth or food, and I withdrew.
(takes a moment to recover) Later in the evening, the
young man began to utter monotonous sounds,
unlike the old man's instrument or the birds'
songs.

(reading aloud under)

I knew nothing then of the science of words or letters; I since found that he read aloud.

Nothing could exceed the love and respect that
the young cottagers displayed toward the old man,
who, I soon saw, was blind. Yet they were not entirely happy, and often went apart and wept. If
such lovely creatures were miserable, it was less
strange that I, imperfect and solitary, should be
wretched. I felt an affinity. What did their tears
imply?

One cause was poverty. They often went hungry,
giving their food to the old man, keeping none for
themselves. Seeing the effect of my stealing from
their store, I stopped, and made do with berries,
nuts, and roots. I also discovered another way to
help them. The youth spent the better part of
each day gathering wood. During the night I took
his tools and brought home fuel for several days.

The first time I did this, they were astonished to see the great pile of wood at the door in the morning. The young man spent that day repairing the cottage and cultivating the garden.

Gradually I discovered they made articulate sounds, words that sometimes produced pleasure or pain, smiles or sadness—a godlike science I ardently wished to learn. But I was baffled, lacking any clue connecting the words with any visible objects. Over several revolutions of the moon, I learned *fire, milk, bread,* and *wood.* The old man has only one name, *father.* The girl, *sister,* or *Agatha;* the youth *Felix, brother,* or *son.*

When they were unhappy, I felt depressed; when they rejoiced, I rejoiced with them. The old man often encouraged his children to cast off their melancholy. Agatha responded, but Felix, wrapped in sadness, continued to read aloud, uttering many of the same sounds as when he talked. I conjectured that he found on the paper signs for speech, and I longed to comprehend these also—but how, when I did not even understand the sounds for which they stood as signs? I improved in this science of words, but I knew I had to master their language if they were to overlook my deformity.

(catches sight of his own reflection, starts)

When I first saw myself in the pool, I knew I was the monster others saw! I was despondent, mortified. Even then I did not realize the fatal effects of my . . . difference.

When the sun became warmer and the light longer, food became more plentiful as new plants sprang up in the garden; and these signs of comfort increased daily as the season advanced. My thought, too, quickened—I wanted to know why Felix was so miserable, Agatha so sad.

Foolish wretch! I thought I might restore their happiness. They would be disgusted until my gentle demeanor and conciliating words should win their favor and then their love. And so I doubled my efforts to acquire their language. One night, collecting food for myself and wood for my protectors, I found a leathern portmanteau containing some books. Eagerly I seized the prize—*Paradise Lost, Plutarch's Lives,* and the *Sorrows of Werther.*

I learned from young Werther that adults are like children. They wander about and do not know where they come from nor where they are going. Further, they rarely act from genuine motives, and are governed, as children, by biscuits and cake and the rod. I also learned that many have observed that life is but a dream.

Werther's disquisitions upon suicide filled me with wonder, and I wept over his death. *(pulling out a torn page, smoothing it)*: ". . . he will create a world from within for himself, and be happy because he is a man. And then, confined as he may be, he . . . still preserves in his heart the sweet sensation of freedom, and the knowledge that he can quit this prison whenever he wishes." Such nobility!

As I read, I applied much to my own feelings and condition, similar yet unlike to the beings about whom I read. Who was I? Whence did I come? What was my destination? These questions continually recurred, but I had no idea how to answer them.

Plutarch elevated me above the wretched sphere of my own reflections to admire and love the heroes of past ages. Oh, how can I describe what rose in my heart? The greatest ardor for virtue, the deepest abhorrence for vice filled my being.

And then, in *Paradise Lost*, an omnipotent God warring with his creatures aroused my awe. Like Adam, I had no link to any other being; but he had come forth from the hands of God a perfect creature, happy and prosperous, while I was helpless and alone.

VICTOR: I never pretended to be God. I never—

CREATURE: Sometimes I considered Satan, not Adam, a fitter emblem of my condition.

VICTOR: Far fitter!

CREATURE: And then, confirming those feelings, I found your journal of the four months preceding my creation in the pocket of the coat I had taken from your laboratory. I sickened as I read. Hateful day when I received life! Why did you form a monster so hideous that even you reject me?

VICTOR: I did not intend it so, I thought only for the good of humankind!

CREATURE: God made man beautiful and alluring, after his own image. Even Satan had his companions, but I am solitary and abhorred. Still, I resolved not to despair but to rely on the cottagers. I had since learned the secret of their sorrows when an Arabian woman, Safie, joined them. Her father had suffered unjust imprisonment in Paris, and Felix had risked his all to free the man. This deed caused the downfall of the family, but now, with Safie, his beloved, restored to him, their melancholy lifted.

(music)

I felt indebted to Safie, because Felix taught her language and history, which I learned as well. And I felt a deeper bond with the family upon learning that they too had suffered injustice. One day when the young people went out for a walk, leaving the old man to his guitar, I summoned my courage and approached the door.

(music stops)

DELACEY: Who is there?

CREATURE: A traveler needing rest. If you would allow me to stop before your fire.

DELACEY: I will do what I can. My children are away, and I am blind. Procuring food will be difficult.

CREATURE: I have food. I need only warmth and rest. I am about to claim the protection of friends, whom I love, and in whose favor I hope. I have no friend or relation on earth. These people to whom I go have never seen me. I am afraid, for if I fail, I am an outcast in the world forever.

DELACEY: Do not despair. To be friendless is indeed unfortunate, but men's hearts can be full of charity. Rely on your hopes.

CREATURE: My life has been hitherto harmless and in some degree beneficial. But a fatal prejudice clouds my friends' eyes—where they should see a friend, they behold only a monster.

DELACEY: If you really are blameless, can you not undeceive them?

CREATURE: I have for many months anonymously done acts of kindness daily for them. But they believe I wish to injure them, and I must overcome that prejudice.

DELACEY: Where do they reside?

CREATURE: Near here.

DELACEY: I cannot judge your countenance, but your words persuade me that you are sincere. If you would confide in me, I may be useful to you.

CREATURE: Excellent man! Your kindness raises me from the dust. By your aid, I trust I shall not be driven from the society and sympathy of your fellows.

DELACEY: Heaven forbid! Even if you were a criminal, for that can only drive you to desperation. I and my family also are unfortunate, condemned, though innocent; therefore I feel for your misfortunes.

CREATURE: How can I thank you? From your lips I have heard the voice of kindness. Your humanity assures me of success.

DELACEY: What are your friends' names and residence?

CREATURE: Answering you means the loss or gain of happiness forever! Oh!

DELACEY: I hear my children returning—perhaps they will—

CREATURE: Now is the time! Save and protect me! You and your family are the friends whom I seek! Do not desert me in my hour of trial!

DELACEY: Good God—who are you?

CREATURE: The children entered, Agatha fainted, Safie rushed out. Felix tore me from his father, dashed me to the ground, and struck me with a stick. I could have torn him limb from limb as the lion rends the antelope, but my heart sank, and I refrained. In the tumult I escaped unperceived to my hovel.

(howls several times)

My protectors departed and thus broke the only link that held me to the world. Unable to injure anything human, I turned my fury toward inanimate objects. I placed combustibles around the cottage. A fierce wind tore along like a mighty avalanche and produced a kind of insanity in my spirits that burst all bounds of reason and reflection. Waiting until the moon had sunk, I waved a lighted brand and fired the straw, heath, and bushes I had collected.

(conflagration)

I flew the scene, intent upon finding my father, my creator—to whom could I apply more fittingly than to him who had given me life? I directed my steps toward Geneva, resting during the day, traveling under cover of night. One morning near a deep, rapid river, a young girl slipped, and she fell into the stream. I rushed from my hiding place and dragged her to shore, where she lay senseless. A rustic tore the girl from my arms. When I followed, he shot me in the shoulder and escaped through the wood.

This then was the reward of my benevolence! Daily I vowed revenge. Reaching Geneva, I slept, waking to the approach of a beautiful child who ran into the recess I had chosen. This creature was too young to recognize deformity. If I could educate him as my companion, I should not be so desolate.

(A child's scream. Lights pick up William.)

I will not hurt you! Listen!

WILLIAM: Let me go! Monster! Wretch! You want to eat me and tear me to pieces! Ogre! Let me go, or I will tell my papa!

CREATURE: You must come with me.

WILLIAM: My papa is a syndic—Monsieur Frankenstein—he will punish you!

CREATURE: Frankenstein! You belong then to my enemy! Upon whom I have sworn eternal revenge! You shall be my first victim!

(lights out on William)

The rest you must have pieced together by now. I took the portrait from his breast and hid in a barn where a young woman was sleeping. "Awake, fairest, thy lover is near—he would give his life to obtain one look of affection." She stirred—would she see me, and curse me, and denounce me? No, no, not I but she shall suffer! The murder that I have committed because I am forever robbed of companionship she shall atone! Thanks to the history lessons of Felix and the sanguinary laws of man, I had learned how to work mischief. I slipped the portrait into the folds of her dress.

(lights up on Justine, hanged)

I am alone and miserable. One as deformed as myself would not deny herself to me. My companion, of the same species and the same defects, you must create.

(lights out on Justine)

VICTOR: I refuse.

CREATURE: I beg you, have mercy! I am malicious because I am miserable. We shall be monsters, but on that account more attached to one another.

VICTOR: I cannot!

CREATURE: Do not deny me! I swear to you, we shall quit the neighborhood of man and dwell in the most savage places. My evil passions will flee when I meet with sympathy, and when I die I will not curse my maker.

VICTOR: You swear to be harmless.

CREATURE: My vices are the children of a forced solitude that I abhor; my virtues will necessarily rise when I live in communion with an equal.

VICTOR: As soon as I deliver a companion—

CREATURE: You will do it?!

VICTOR: Who will go with you in your exile—

CREATURE: You will give me a mate?

VICTOR: If I do, you must swear to quit Europe forever—

CREATURE: I swear!

VICTOR: And every other place in the neighborhood of man—

CREATURE: By the sun, and by the blue sky of heaven, and by the fire of love that burns my heart! By all these, I swear!

VICTOR: Then—I will—apply myself.

CREATURE: Oh! You are merciful!

VICTOR: Please!

CREATURE: And when you are ready, I shall be there.

VICTOR: Oh! What have I done?! Would that I might disappear! Stars, winds—leave me in darkness! *(disappears)*

Scene 2

Victor at loose ends, staring into the fire; Alphonse eyes him for a moment.

ALPHONSE: You are returning to yourself. Yet you are still unhappy, still avoiding society. The other day I thought I knew why. I hope you will confirm my supposition if I am correct.

(Victor turns away, afraid of what might be coming)

I have always assumed that you and Elizabeth would marry. She has long been your sister—you may not wish her to become your wife. You may even have another in mind.

VICTOR: Please, Father, you may—

ALPHONSE: And, feeling honor-bound to Elizabeth, you are caught in a dilemma, struggling to break free, clearly miserable—

VICTOR: Please! Father! Reassure yourself! I love Elizabeth and hope that my future is bound up with hers.

ALPHONSE: I cannot tell you how happy this makes me! Why suffer this gloom a moment longer? Let the marriage go forward now.

VICTOR: My studies. . . .

ALPHONSE: All as you wish. Speak freely, please.

VICTOR: *(to himself)* If only I could! I have a promise to keep. *(to Alphonse)* In my heart, Father, I want to marry immediately. There is one impediment, however—some business in England that cannot wait. A few months, at most a year, then I shall return and marry.

ALPHONSE: If this journey rouses you from your melancholy, Victor, I am glad for it. Come back to us restored! *(leaving)* Your union with Elizabeth will gladden my waning years.

HENRY: *(entering)* Oh, my dear friend! Have you ever seen such natural beauty? This is what it is to live! Now I enjoy existence!

VICTOR: If I could say the same!

HENRY: I have seen the most beautiful scenes of my own country, the lakes of Lucerne and Uri, the mountains of La Valais, the Pays de Vaud; but this country, Victor, pleases me more than all these wonders. Yes, the mountains of Switzerland are more majestic, but this divine river has unequaled charm. Look at that castle overhanging the precipice; another on the island, nearly hidden by foliage; those laborers coming from their vines; that village half concealed in the mountain's recess. Surely the soul of the spirit that inhabits this place moves more harmoniously with man than those of the glaciers or inaccessible peaks of our own country!

VICTOR: You yourself are formed in the poetry of nature, your wild imagination chastened by your heart, your friendship devoted.

HENRY: ". . . a feeling, and a love,
That had no need of a remoter charm,
By thought supplied, or any interest
Unborrow'd from the eye."

You must have a care for your own well-being.

VICTOR: I feel—distanced from humankind. Oh, Henry! I see the blood of William, of Justine.

HENRY: Travel! Travel will restore your peace of mind!

VICTOR: *(to himself)* He is always over my shoulder. Oh, may I satisfy him! *(to Henry)* I am unfit for civilized society, Henry. Better I finish my tour alone.

HENRY: I'd rather be with you in your solitary rambles than with people I do not know.

VICTOR: Please, enjoy yourself—I will return, I hope, with a lighter heart—more like your own.

HENRY: Hurry—for in your absence I cannot feel at home.

(eerie moonlight as Victor repeats earlier business with the mannekins)

VICTOR: Oh, God! What am I doing?! Three years ago, I created a fiend who has desolated my heart and filled it forever with the most bitter remorse. Now I am forming another being who may become ten thousand times more malignant than her mate—who may delight in murder! She has not sworn to quit the company of mankind! She may refuse. They may, further, hate each other. He loathes his own deformity—can he not conceive even greater abhorrence of hers? He may, in turn, disgust her. Worse, propagate a race of devils. Oh! My promise is all wickedness!

(lights pick up Creature)

CREATURE: Forgive my intrusion. I am merely marking your progress.

VICTOR: You are malicious!

72

CREATURE: I claim your promise.

VICTOR: How can I have agreed to your condition?

(trembling, Victor tears the thing to pieces)

CREATURE: You dare? Fool!

(The Creature howls and rushes off. A bundle flies aloft, another corpse joining William and Justine. Blackout. Sounds of the sea, perhaps bell, or foghorn, as moonlight picks up Victor. The creaking of a door as lights also pick up Creature. Victor, frozen in terror, awaits some awful pronouncement.)

CREATURE: You dare to break your promise?! I have endured misery, creeping over the shores of the Rhine, dwelling among the heaths of England, suffering fatigue and cold and hunger—and you dare to destroy my hopes?!

VICTOR: I do, I do! Go! I will never create another like you, deformed, wicked—never!

CREATURE: Slave! I am your master—obey!

VICTOR: I am resolved. I will never set loose upon the earth another demon who delights in death and wretchedness, one with whom you can propagate a race of monsters. However ambivalent I have felt, I am determined on this course. Go!

CREATURE: Shall I be alone? All, all alone? I was affectionate but met only detestation and scorn. Are you to be happy while I am condemned to grovel in the intensity of my wretchedness? Blast all my other passions, my revenge remains, henceforth dearer than light or food!

VICTOR: Stop! Your words cannot make me bend.

73

CREATURE: I shall be with you on your wedding night.

VICTOR: Villain! Before you sign my death warrant, secure your own safety.

(As Victor lunges forward, the Creature disappears. Sounds of the sea, and the Creature's voice echoing, "I will be with you on your wedding night." Victor packs up the remains of the second creature. Sounds of the sea, wind, and waves.)

VICTOR: If the sea be my grave, then fiend, your task is fulfilled!

(Wind and waves subsiding. Villagers emerging from the shadows.)

VICTOR: My good friends! Where am I? What town is this?

MAN 1: You'll find out soon enough. It may or may not suit your taste, but you've got no say in your quarters.

VICTOR: Why do you answer so roughly? Surely the English honor hospitality?

MAN 2: The English do what they do. The Irish hate villains.

VICTOR: I knew I was off course. But Ireland! Would someone have the kindness to direct me to an inn?

MAN 1: You must come to Mr. Kirwin to account for yourself.

VICTOR: Why? Is this not a free country?

MAN 2: For honest folks. But last night we found a gentleman murdered here, and the magistrate needs a word with you.

MAN 1: Last night, fishing with my son and brother-in-law, a strong blast blew up, and we put in for port. Walking from the harbor, I stumbled and fell over a man's corpse.

MAN 2: We first thought he'd drowned, but his clothes were dry, and his body still warm. Young fellow, strangled. Black marks around his neck.

WOMAN 1: I saw a boat push off from the spot where you found the body.

MAN 2: And I saw the same boat this fellow landed in, just off shore, before we found the corpse.

WOMAN 2: Still warm it was. We sent for the apothecary—too late.

MAGISTRATE: *(lifting the sheet from the corpse)* There, sir.

VICTOR: I am not sure I can look. *(collects himself, looks, inhales sharply)* My dearest Henry! Two already destroyed, others await their destiny, but you, my friend, Henry, my benefactor—

MAGISTRATE: There, now, sir—

VICTOR: I murdered William, Justine, Henry! Help me destroy the fiend! *(gasping)* Help! He is choking me! Stop—I can't—help me!

(Blackout. Lights slowly up.)

WOMAN: Are you better now, sir?

VICTOR: I . . . think so. Although . . . if this was no dream . . . I dread being alive, the misery, the horror.

WOMAN: Oh, you're right there. You'd be better off dead, for they say it will go hard with you.

VICTOR: Do they now.

75

WOMAN: None of my concern, of course. I'm only to nurse you, get you well. I do my duty with a clear conscience. World'd be a better place if more could say the same.

VICTOR: What news? What new scene of death? Whose am I now to lament?

MAGISTRATE: Your family is well. And someone come to visit.

VICTOR: Oh! Take him away! I cannot see him! Do not let him in!

MAGISTRATE: I should have expected you to welcome your father with—

VICTOR: My father! Where is he? *(turning to him)* You are safe! And—Elizabeth?

ALPHONSE: All well, asking for your health, dear Victor. *(glancing about)* What a wretched place! What fatality pursues you? Poor Henry.

VICTOR: Yes, Father—some horrible destiny hangs over me, and I must live to fulfill it. Or else I should have died on Henry's coffin.

MAGISTRATE: The grand jury has rejected the bill, since the evidence clearly shows you to be in the Orkneys when the body was found.

ALPHONSE: You are free, Victor—we must leave for Geneva.

VICTOR: *(to himself)* Dungeon or palace is equally hateful. Everything is dark, frightening. Henry's eyes languish in death. The monster's watery gaze. The fiend at my throat! *(groaning)* Ah!

(lights dim on Victor, come up on Alphonse)

ALPHONSE: Victor, I have done everything I can to help you slough off these melancholy moods. You mustn't give way to despair. Or misplaced shame. Having to answer the charge of murder has weighed you down with a sense of disgrace. But you must put that behind you.

VICTOR: Justine was as innocent as I, yet she both suffered the same charge and died for it.

ALPHONSE: Yes, well, we all regret that, but we—

VICTOR: I! I am the cause! I murdered her!

ALPHONSE: Victor, please, calm yourself.

VICTOR: William, Justine, Henry—they all died by my hands.

ALPHONSE: Please, my dearest Victor—you are over-wrought. What is this delusion that grips you?

VICTOR: May the sun and the heavens bear me witness! I am the assassin of these innocents.

ALPHONSE: There now, my son. You must rest.

VICTOR: A thousand times I would have shed my blood, drop by drop, if I could have saved their lives.

ALPHONSE: You must calm these wild imaginings.

VICTOR: But I could not, Father, I could not! Indeed, I could not save the whole human race.

ALPHONSE: We will ignore them. We will not speak of them again.

(Victor opens a letter as Elizabeth seals an envelope and approaches him)

ELIZABETH: My dear friend, how much you have suffered! Yet I hope to see peace in your countenance and to find that your heart retains some comfort and tranquility. I would not disturb you, but a conversation I had with my uncle makes an explanation necessary before we meet.

I dare not delay any longer writing what I have often wished to express but have lacked the courage to say. Since we were infants, your parents desired our union. Yet, just as brother and sister often feel a lively affection without desiring a more intimate union, may this not also be true of us? Answer me with simple truth. Do you not love another?

VICTOR: Sweet and beloved Elizabeth!

ELIZABETH: When I saw you last autumn, so unhappy, flying to solitude, I supposed you might regret our connection, yet feel honor-bound to fulfill your parents' wishes. I confess I love you.

VICTOR: Oh, my dear!

ELIZABETH: Yet you must freely choose to marry, Victor, be assured, be happy. And if you accede to this request, nothing will interrupt my tranquility, whether or not we marry. If I know you are happy, I shall need no other happiness.

(Lights fade on Elizabeth as the Creature's voice echoes: "I will be with you on your wedding night!")

VICTOR: So be it! If you kill me, I will be at peace. If I kill you, I will be free!

CREATURE: You dare to hope for the happiness you have denied me!

VICTOR: Adrift, homeless, penniless, and alone, but free. With my treasure, Elizabeth, to help me endure my remorse and guilt! And yet you may strike any time. Why should I postpone? *(writing)* "All I may one day enjoy is centered in you."

ELIZABETH: *(reading)* "Chase away your fears: to you alone do I consecrate my life and my endeavors for contentment."

VICTOR: "I . . . have one secret, Elizabeth, a dreadful one. . . ."

ELIZABETH: "I will confide this tale the day after our marriage, for there must be perfect confidence between us. . . ."

ALPHONSE: Let us cling closer to what remains and transfer our love for those lost to those who yet live. Our circle will be small but bound by the ties of affection and mutual misfortune. And when time shall have softened your despair, new and clear objects of care will be born to replace those torn from us.

CREATURE: I will be with you. . . .

(Sounds of horses pulling a carriage through deserted streets. Victor and Elizabeth on their honeymoon.)

VICTOR: You are sorrowful, my love. If you knew what I have suffered and may yet endure, you would try to encourage the freedom from despair this one day allows me.

ELIZABETH: If lively joy is not painted in my face, my heart is contented. Something whispers not to depend too much on the prospect before us, but I refuse to listen to such a sinister voice. How quickly the current carries us! And how the clouds now obscure, now reveal the peak of Mont Blanc. And the fish, swimming in waters so clear we can make out every pebble at the bottom!

Such a divine day! How happy and serene nature seems!

VICTOR: Seems. Yes.

(winds come up, and a rainstorm descends)

ELIZABETH: What agitates you, Victor? What is it you fear?

VICTOR: Peace, peace, my love. I am a nervous bridegroom.

ELIZABETH: And I a nervous bride.

VICTOR: After this night, all will be safe. But this night is dreadful, very dreadful. Please—you must retire. I will join you soon.

ELIZABETH: I cannot leave you in such a state.

VICTOR: Please do as I say. I will explain everything to you in the morning. *(kisses her)* Good night.

ELIZABETH: Good night. *(leaves)*

VICTOR: *(sets out a dagger on the table, and draws a pistol)* I will watch, and pray, and if he appears, I will—

(a bloodcurdling scream)

My God! No!

(lights pick up Elizabeth's corpse)

Why am I left alive? Only to relate the destruction of the best hope and purest creature on earth?

MARY: She was there—

VICTOR: lifeless and inanimate—

MARY: thrown across the bed—

VICTOR: her head hanging down—

MARY AND VICTOR: and her pale and distorted features half covered by her hair.

VICTOR: Everywhere I turn I see the same figure—her bloodless arms and relaxed form flung by the murderer on its bridal bier. *(embracing her)*

(A montage of the murdered—William, Justine, Henry. Victor looks up to see the Creature at the casement.)

CREATURE: Grieve! Rage! As I when you destroyed—

(Victor shoots. The Creature disappears.)

VICTOR: Elizabeth! Elizabeth!

(blackout)

Scene 3

Sounds of the sea.

VICTOR: You must add one more death to the list. When my father lost his charm and his delight— his Elizabeth, his more than daughter, whom he doted on with all that affection that a man feels, who in the decline of life, having few affections, clings more earnestly to those that remain. The springs of existence suddenly gave way, and in a few days he died in my arms. It was then I determined to pursue my destroyer to death.

MAGISTRATE: Be assured, sir, we shall spare no pains to discover the villain.

VICTOR: The story is too connected to be mistaken for a dream, and I have no motive for falsehood. It is your duty as a magistrate to exert your whole power.

MAGISTRATE: I would afford you every aid in your pursuit, but how would this be a match for such powers? Who could follow such an animal? Besides, months have elapsed—he could be anywhere.

VICTOR: I am sure he hovers nearby, and if he has taken refuge in the Alps, he may be hunted like the chamois and destroyed as a beast of prey. But you doubt my narrative.

MAGISTRATE: You are mistaken.

VICTOR: You do not intend to pursue my enemy.

MAGISTRATE: If we can seize him, he shall suffer proportionate punishment. Even so, you should prepare to accept disappointment.

VICTOR: Never. You refuse my just demand: I have but one resource, and I devote myself, either in my life or death, to his destruction.

MAGISTRATE: Control yourself, and consider. Your story has certain elements of—delirium.

VICTOR: How ignorant you are in the pride of your wisdom! Say no more, for you know not what you say.

(Cemetery. Sounds of rustling leaves; some flickering shadows; owls hooting. Victor kneels, and kisses the ground.)

VICTOR: By the sacred earth, by the shades that wander near me, by my deep and eternal grief, I swear; and by thee, O Night, and the spirits that preside over thee, to pursue the demon until he or I shall perish in mortal conflict. For this purpose I will preserve my life. To execute this dear revenge will I again behold the sun and tread the green herbage of earth, which otherwise would vanish from my eyes forever.

(A fiendish but almost imperceptible laugh. Victor looks around for a moment, decides his ears deceive him, resumes.)

I call on you, spirits of the dead, and on you, wandering ministers of vengeance, to aid and conduct me in my work. Let the cursed and hellish monster drink deep of agony; let him feel the despair that now torments me.

(The fiendish laugh rings out, echoes. Victor starts up, looking around. The laugh recedes.)

CREATURE: *(reverberating whisper)* I am satisfied, miserable wretch. You have determined to live, and I am satisfied.

VICTOR: I will follow the windings of the Rhone to the blue Mediterranean, to the Black Sea, amidst the wilds of Tartary and Russia.

Sometimes the peasants, scared by this horrid apparition, inform me of his path; sometimes he himself leaves some mark to guide me. I am cursed by some devil, and I carry with me my eternal hell; yet still a spirit of good follows and directs my steps. When hunger overcomes me and I sink under exhaustion, a coarse repast, such as the local peasants eat, appears, set there, I will not doubt, by the spirits I invoke to aid me. When all is dry, the heavens cloudless, and I am parched by thirst, clouds bedim the sky, shed the few drops that revive me, and vanish. During sleep alone I taste joy.

ELIZABETH: *(reverberating whisper)* Your cousin and playmate ... too sincere a love ... nothing on earth shall disturb my tranquility. ...

(Each of these dream speeches repeats under as the next

one picks up. The effect should be soothing and benign, even musically appealing.)

JUSTINE: *(ditto)* In heaven, where we shall all be happy.

ALPHONSE: *(ditto)* Cling closer . . . transfer our love to those who yet live.

HENRY: *(ditto)* The noble art of bookkeeping! Together we shall undertake the voyage of discovery to the land of knowledge!

MARY (AS CAROLINE): *(ditto)* . . . to resign myself cheerfully to death and indulge a hope of meeting you in another world.

VICTOR: Sometimes they haunted even my waking hours and persuaded me that they still lived! Then vengeance died in my heart, and I pursued the demon more as a task enjoined by heaven than as the ardent desire of my soul.

CREATURE: My reign is not yet over. You live, and my power is complete. Follow me to the everlasting ices of the north, where you will feel the misery of cold and frost to which I am impervious.

VICTOR: Scoffing devil!

CREATURE: You will find a dead hare—eat and be refreshed.

VICTOR: Vengeance, torture, and death.

CREATURE: Come on, my enemy—we have yet to wrestle for our lives.

VICTOR: And then I shall join Elizabeth and my friends in the reward of this tedious and horrible pilgrimage!

84

CREATURE: Your toils only begin! Wrap yourself in furs and provide food. Soon your sufferings will satisfy my everlasting hatred.

VICTOR: Heaven, support me. How unlike the blue seasons of the south! Covered with ice, the ocean was only to be distinguished from land by its superior wildness and ruggedness. The Greeks wept for joy when they beheld the Mediterranean from the hills of Asia and hailed with rapture the boundary of their toils. I did not weep. *(kneels)* Thank you, guiding spirit, for conducting me safely. Let me intercept him before he can reach the beach! *(rising, defeated)* Too late. He had arrived the night before.

WOMAN: With a gun, and many pistols!

MAN: Took our food, dogs, sledge.

WOMAN: And went off across the sea!

MAN: Where, mark my words, he'll freeze to death.

WOMAN: Or the ice will break him!

(the fiendish laugh echoes)

VICTOR: Not he!

(Elizabeth, Alphonse, Henry, Justine, William appear variously, their whispers reverberating, fragmented, and continuing under until they fade out)

ALPHONSE: Bound by ties of affection. . . .

WILLIAM: My papa will punish you!

JUSTINE: Think of me as one unjustly condemned.

HENRY: Hasten, my dear friend—I cannot feel at home in your absence.

ELIZABETH: My heart is contented.

VICTOR: I lack stamina. I must give it up. *(sees something, cries out ecstatically)* No more than a mile distant!

(Wind and sea, storm rising and prevailing. Terrible sounds, as of an earthquake. Lights up on Captain Walton.)

VICTOR: It was all over in a few minutes. And I was left drifting on a scattered piece of ice that was continually lessening and thus preparing me for a hideous death. But after many appalling hours I saw your vessel riding at anchor, and—

CAPTAIN WALTON: And the rest I know.

VICTOR: Must I die, and he yet live? Oh, swear, Walton, that he shall not live. He is eloquent and persuasive; and once his words had power over my heart: but trust him not. Hear him not! Call on William, Justine, Henry, Elizabeth, my father, and the wretched Victor, and thrust your sword into his heart. I will hover near and direct the steel aright. Swear to me, Walton, that he shall not live.

CAPTAIN WALTON: I would give anything to know the particulars of the Creature's formation.

VICTOR: Are you mad? Do you realize where your endless curiosity will lead? Peace. Learn from my miseries—so that you will not increase your own.

CAPTAIN WALTON: I have learned.

VICTOR: That way madness lies.

CAPTAIN WALTON: How I wish I could comfort you.

VICTOR: Cold comfort. I find comfort only in my dreams. When I was younger, I thought I was destined for greatness. I thought I would achieve a great work. Above all, I wanted to be useful to my fellows. When I thought about my creation—a sensitive and rational animal, I ranked myself above the herd. And this thought buoyed me at the beginning of my career. Now, however! It plunges me into despair. All my aspirations are nothing. And like the archangel who aspired to omnipotence, I am another Lucifer, chained in an eternal hell. Oh, my friend, if you had known me as I once was, you would not recognize me as I am now.

CAPTAIN WALTON: Please do not say such things. You must take heart. I feel as if I have just found in you the friend I had longed for. You must sustain your spirits. You must reconcile yourself to life.

VICTOR: I appreciate your feelings. But do you really think I can form new ties of affection, plagued as I am with thoughts of those who are gone? Can any man be another Henry? Any woman another Elizabeth? What's more, later friendships can hardly touch those formed when we were children. Wherever I am, the soothing voice of Elizabeth, the conversation of Henry, will be ever in my ear. They are dead. And I am bereft. I would preserve my life only if I were engaged in some high design that promised to be useful to my fellow human beings. That, however, is not my destiny. I am not meant to fulfill such an undertaking but rather to destroy the being to whom I gave life. Then, then I will have finished my appointed task and will be freed by death to join my childhood friends.

CAPTAIN WALTON: *(writing)* My Beloved Sister: These papers may never reach you; yet I am compelled to record the scene. We are still surrounded by mountains of ice, still in imminent danger of being crushed. In the excessive cold and desolation, many of my comrades have found graves.

Frankenstein declines daily, although his eyes still glimmer with a feverish fire. This morning, as I watched my friend, half a dozen sailors demanded admission into the cabin.

LEADER: Captain, we have little hope that we shall escape this desolate place. On the slender chance that the ice might dissipate, the men have asked me to present their case. If we are freed, you must agree to direct your course immediately southward.

CAPTAIN WALTON: Have you all lost faith in our enterprise?

LEADER: To continue north would be madness. You risk even further loss of life.

CAPTAIN WALTON: I will not despair!

LEADER: Despair! We will gladly exchange fond hope for certain justice.

CAPTAIN WALTON: I had rather die than return shamefully.

LEADER: But we would rather live.

CAPTAIN WALTON: Under any circumstances?

LEADER: We feel no shame at being trapped in these mountains of ice.

VICTOR: Are you so easily turned from your design? Hereafter you were to be hailed as the benefactors of your species, brave men who encountered death for the benefit of mankind. And now—with the first trial of your courage, you are content to be handed down as those poor souls who were chilly and returned to their warm firesides. Be men, or be more than men! Steady to your purpose, firm as rock. This ice is not made of such stuff as your hearts. It is mutable and cannot withstand you if you say that it shall not. Do not return to your families with the stigma of disgrace etched into your brows. Return as heroes who have fought and conquered.

CAPTAIN WALTON: We will all benefit from time to consider what has been said.

LEADER: What shall we tell the others?

CAPTAIN WALTON: I will not lead you north if you refuse to be so led. I hope, however, upon reflection, your courage will again sustain you.

(Sound of ice cracking, wind rising. Several joyful shouts.)

VICTOR: What is happening?

CAPTAIN WALTON: We are returning to England. I cannot lead them into danger. I must return.

VICTOR: You may give up your purpose, but mine is assigned to me by heaven.

CAPTAIN WALTON: You are weak.

VICTOR: The spirits who assist my vengeance will strengthen me.

(trying to rise, he falls back)

CAPTAIN WALTON: The surgeon gave him a composing draught and told me he had not many hours to live.

VICTOR: I shall soon die, while my enemy and persecutor—! I no longer feel the burning hatred I once felt, Walton. But I do feel justified in desiring my adversary's death. In my enthusiastic madness I created a rational creature and was bound to assure, insofar as I could, his happiness and well-being. Yet I had another, paramount duty—my own species had greater claims because they included a greater proportion of happiness or misery. So I refused to create a companion for the first creature. He showed unparalleled evil and malignity. He destroyed my friends. He ought to die, yet I have failed in his destruction. That he should live disturbs me. In other respects, this hour, as I expect any moment my release, is the only happy one I have enjoyed for several years.

(lights pick up Elizabeth, Henry, Alphonse, William, Justine)

I hasten to your arms! Farewell, Walton! Seek happiness in tranquility and avoid ambition, even distinguishing yourself in science and discoveries.

(Silence. Victor tries to speak, cannot, presses Captain Walton's hand.)

CAPTAIN WALTON: Oh, Margaret! How can I comment on the untimely death of this glorious spirit? What can I say to convey the depth of my sorrow? But I journey toward England—I may there find consolation.

(Lights fade. Perhaps some music. Lights pick up Creature bending over body of Victor, uttering sounds of grief. Hearing Captain Walton, the Creature springs toward the window.)

Wait! Stay!

(After a moment, the Creature turns toward Victor, speaking in a "suffocated" voice)

CREATURE: You, too, are my victim! In your murder, my crimes are consummated! My miserable being has wound to its close!

CAPTAIN WALTON: *(to himself)* As was his fervent hope!

CREATURE: Oh, Frankenstein! Generous and self-devoted being! To what avail do I now ask you to pardon me? I, who irretrievably destroyed you by destroying all you loved.

CAPTAIN WALTON: Your repentance is superfluous.

CREATURE: *(touching Victor, recoiling)* Ah! he is cold! He cannot answer me.

CAPTAIN WALTON: Too late now the voice of conscience, the sting of remorse!

CREATURE: *(turning to Captain Walton)* You think I have been dead to agony and remorse? A frightful selfishness hurried me on while my heart was poisoned with remorse! Do you think Henry's groans were music to my ears? My heart was inclined toward love and sympathy. And when misery twisted that same heart toward vice and hatred, the violence of the change was torture.

CAPTAIN WALTON: Wretch! You throw a torch into a pile of buildings, and when they are consumed you sit among the ruins and lament the fall.

CREATURE: After Henry's murder, I returned to Switzerland, heartbroken. I pitied Frankenstein, and I abhorred myself. But once I discovered he hoped for that happiness he himself had denied me, then envy fed vengeance. I was the slave, not the master, detesting my impulse but bound to obey it.

CAPTAIN WALTON: Hypocritical fiend! If Frankenstein were alive, he would again be the prey of your accursed vengeance.

CREATURE: Yet when she died! Evil became my good. I adapted my nature to what I had chosen. Completing the design became my passion. And now it is ended—there is my last victim!

CAPTAIN WALTON: You feel no pity—only regret that your victim lies beyond your reach.

CREATURE: Oh, not thus ... not thus. I know I may never find sympathy. I first sought fellow feeling because I overflowed with happiness, affection, and the love of virtue. I longed to participate with others. But now! Now virtue is mere shadow, happiness and affection turned to bitter loathing and despair—in what should I seek for sympathy? Once I falsely hoped to meet with beings who would pardon my outward form and love me for my excellence. But now. Now, crime has cast me below the meanest animal. No guilt, no malignity, no misery compares to mine. The fallen angel becomes the malignant devil. Yet even Lucifer had friends in his desolation: I am alone.

While I dashed his hopes, I failed to fulfill my own desires. I sought love and fellowship but was spurned. Was this justice? Am I the only criminal, when humankind sinned against me? Why not hate Felix, who drove me from the door? Why not execrate the rustic who tried to destroy his child's savior? But they are virtuous, immaculate, and I am an abortion. *(cries out in frustration)*

And, nonetheless, a wretch. I have strangled the innocent, asleep, and grasped the throat of one who never injured me or any other human being. I have devoted my creator, the select specimen of all that is worthy of love and admiration among men, to misery. *(moves toward Victor)* White and cold, like ice, in death.

(turning to Captain Walton) Your hatred cannot equal my own for myself. My heart conceived the act. My hands executed the deed. Oh, how I long for the moment when I will see these hands and no longer be haunted by their history! Only one task remains.

(Captain Walton starts, or cries out)

Not your death—or any man's except my own. At the northernmost extremity of the globe, I shall collect my funeral pyre and immolate my miserable frame, leaving no remains to enlighten any curious and unhallowed wretch who would create another such as I have been. I shall no longer see the sun or stars or feel the winds play on my cheeks. Some years ago, when the world first opened to me and I felt the cheering warmth of summer and heard the rustling of the leaves and the warbling of the birds, these were all to me: I should have wept to die. Now death is my only consolation.

(to Captain Walton) Farewell. Farewell, Frankenstein. You sought my extinction that I might cause no further wretchedness. Yet, blasted as you were, my agony overshadowed yours. Remorse rankles bitterly in my wounds until death shall close them forever. Soon I shall exult in the torturing flames. The light will fade, the winds will sweep my ashes into the sea, my spirit will sleep in peace.

Or—if it thinks—surely it will not think thus.

Farewell.

(Lights fade on Captain Walton as the Creature ascends toward fire. Music. Mary blows out the candle.)

St. Louis Community College
at Meramec
Library